THE MANDALA WORKBOOK
CREATING AN AUTHENTIC SPIRITUAL PATH

AN INTERSPIRITUAL PROCESS

THE MANDALA WORKBOOK
CREATING AN AUTHENTIC SPIRITUAL PATH

AN INTERSPIRITUAL PROCESS

Edward W. Bastian, Ph.D.

Albion
Andalus
Boulder, Colorado
2016

"The old shall be renewed,
and the new shall be made holy."
– Rabbi Avraham Yitzhak Kook

Albion-Andalus, Inc.
P. O. Box 19852
Boulder, CO 80308
www.albionandalus.com

Spiritual Styles Profile Instrument™ and Spiritual Questions Profile Instrument™ are registered Trade Marks (™ 2013) of Edward W. Bastian, Ph.D.
Spiritual Styles Mandala is a registered Trade Mark ™ of Edward W. Bastian, Ph.D.
Design and composition by Samantha Krezinski, Albion-Andalus Inc.
Cover design by Sari Wisenthal-Shore, Sari Design
The "Flower of InterSpiritual Meditation" envisioned by Edward W. Bastian and created by Lynda Rae.
Photos of Edward W. Bastian by Charles Abbott and Michael Stinson.

ISBN-13: 978-0692575857 (Albion-Andalus Books)
ISBN-10: 0692575855

For more information on the Spiritual Paths Institute,

Spiritual Paths seminars, and courses in InterSpiritual Meditation, please

visit www.spiritualpaths.net, www.interspiritualmeditation.org,

or email ed@spiritualpaths.net.

TABLE OF CONTENTS

The Mandala is a circular, geometric pattern, and colorful representation of the wisdom and practices leading to a fully enlightened, actualized state of being. It provides a visual support for manifesting our ultimate human potential. The Mandala Process articulates twelve families of archetypal spiritual styles, questions, and resources. It outlines a process for the development of a personal spiritual path drawn from the wisdom and practices of many traditions.

— Ed Bastian

People say that what we're all seeking is a meaning for life. I don't think that's what we're really seeking. I think that what we're seeking is an experience of being alive, so that our life experience on the purely physical plane will have resonances within out own innermost being and reality, so that we actually feel the rapture of being alive.

— Joseph Campbell, *The Power of Myth*

Only gradually did I discover what the mandala really is: Formation, Transformation, Eternal Mind's eternal recreation. And that is the self, the wholeness of the personality, which if all goes well is harmonious, but which cannot tolerate self-deception.

— C.G. Jung, *Memories, Dreams, Reflections*

PART ONE

INTRODUCTION TO
SPIRITUAL STYLES & QUESTIONS

CREATING YOUR SPIRITUAL PATH

SPIRITUAL STYLES AND QUESTIONS

Your predominate spiritual styles and questions often lay behind the curtain of your conscious awareness.

These styles and questions shape your spiritual views and practices.

Your styles and questions will change over the course of your life.

They are of equal value and change over time.

There is an infinite diversity and combination of styles, questions, and human beings.

The instruments and worksheets herein are designed to help you explore and harness your own styles and questions to create a satisfying and sustainable spiritual path.

THE PROCESS

INQUIRY: discovering, honoring, cultivating and harnessing your archetypal spiritual styles.

INSIGHT: harnessing your styles to find your spiritual answers; practices. Then deepening your insights and practices through InterSpiritual Meditation.

INTEGRATION: applying your spiritual styles, insights and values into your daily life and contemplative practice.

The Benefits

A spiritual path that gives your life meaning, purpose, and direction.

Teachers, resources, and practices that align with your spiritual styles and help answer your questions and create your personal spiritual path.

Consilience among spiritual, psychological, mythological, indigenous, and scientific traditions.

An InterSpiritual appreciation and integration of wisdom and practice from one or more spiritual traditions.

A core set of values, insights, and practices enabling you to "lead from within" as we engage in the challenges of life.

A calm, focused, empathetic, and centered state-of-being.

A method and process for mentoring individuals with diverse spiritual styles, questions, and resources.

A process that can accompany your service to others in such vocations as psychotherapy, healthcare, education, business and public service.

PURPOSE OF THIS WORKBOOK

DURING THE COURSE OF your lifetime, you might have tried to develop a spiritual path by learning from respected teachers, reading books by popular authors, participating in retreats, or listening and watching inspirational audios and videos. Or, you might just be starting off on your journey of spiritual exploration and discovery, and don't know where to begin. Whether you are a seasoned seeker or a new beginner, you might still be aspiring for a mature spiritual path. If so, I hope this Mandala Process will aid you along your journey.

One of the most profound lessons I have learned about the process of education in general, and spiritual development in particular, is the importance of beginning by asking yourself these questions: How do I learn? How do I know? What is my natural learning style? Once you gain this basic level of self-knowledge you will be able to discern the best teacher, educational resources, and spiritual practices for you.

If you don't begin this way, you are likely to fall away from spiritual pursuits because your spiritual learning style did not match up with the teacher or educational processes you have tried. For example, your spiritual interests might be thwarted because you are a kinesthetic learner compelled to sit still with a highly intellectual teacher; or you are a nature lover confined in a room with hours of silent meditation; or you are a mystical learner who is told to memorize lists of religious dogma; or you are an intellectual learner whose teacher requires devotion and prayer without reason. If these are the case, it will be difficult for you to develop a meaningful and sustainable personal spiritual path.

The second thing that I have learned is the importance of formulating your own questions. For once you have refined your questions, or areas of interest, the educational process can truly begin based on your own curiosity rather than the dictums of a one-size-fits-all system of learning.

Therefore, your first job is to discern how you learn in order to engage in the spiritual adventure through the archetypal spiritual styles that are natural for you. Then, through the lens of these natural styles, you can begin anew by re-engaging with the basic spiritual questions that you have had since childhood like: Who am I? What is my purpose? What happens when I die?

By harnessing your archetypal spiritual styles, honoring your questions, and discerning the best practices for you, a satisfying and sustainable spiritual path can then emerge. The Mandala Process will not provide a quick fix, but rather a context and a process for a holistic, life-long inner career. As you gradually create and follow your path, new insights and experiences will continually arise to give meaning, purpose, and satisfaction to your life.

THE MANDALA PROCESS:
INQUIRY – INSIGHT – INTEGRATION

The integration of spiritual insights and values into daily life is a challenge for each of us, just as it has been for our ancestors for thousands of years. Yet, these same ancestors have left us with the legacy of psychological, mythological, philosophical, religious, scientific, and spiritual resources to help guide our journeys. These provide with invaluable foundations for our personal journeys.

The field of psychology helps reveal the inner dynamics of your mind including your emotions, cognitions, perceptions, habits, and personality traits. Mythology helps you to become aware of your inner dynamics through the stories of archetypal beings who personify them in their lives. Philosophy provides a rational framework for finding answers to life's big questions about your existence, the nature of reality, your ways of knowing, and your values. Religions offer teachings, rituals, belief systems, and communities of worship, as well as civilizing principles for governing your thoughts, emotions, habits, and behaviors in relationship with others. Spirituality helps you to experience the essence of your existence, actualize such essential values as love, compassion, empathy, and wisdom, and to reconnect with the original epiphanies and insights upon which a religion was founded.

The Mandala Process is designed to help you reclaim a personal sense of the spiritual and infuse these values and insights into all aspects of your life. It is a process for marrying the treasures of all the world's 'wisdom traditions' to forge greater unity, happiness, and wellbeing amongst us all.

The premise here is that you are predisposed to view spiritual practice through the lens of your own habituated ways-of-being, i.e., your archetypal spiritual styles. These styles define the way you approach spirituality and, therefore, the way in which you craft your own personal path. Your general spiritual paths are the reflections of your unique set of predispositions that influence the ways you perceive and process data of a spiritual nature and then organize this data into spiritual meaning and practice.

This process turns the old model of fitting yourself into rigidly defined religious dogma on its head. Rather than beginning with a set of doctrines and beliefs into which you must fit yourself, this process begins by discerning your natural styles and questions through which you explore and discover the best path for you. The Mandala Process provides a process, not answers. It offers a container, not the truths and practices you put into it.

INQUIRY

The Mandala Process provides a context for the inclusion of a wide variety of approaches to inner development. It provides us with baskets wherein we can collect the knowledge we accumulate over our lives that defines who we are and how we view the essential issues of our existence. It provides a process wherein we can systematically store and retrieve the truths that give our lives meaning. It provides a general outline for life-long *inquiry* into the nature of our existence and the creation of principles around which we choose to live our lives.

INSIGHT

The process of the Mandala Process is further deepened through the contemplative and meditative process contained in the seven steps of InterSpiritual Meditation (ISM). This contemplative process is designed to be customized by each individual according to their personal spiritual styles and questions. ISM provides an individualized, rather than a one-size-fits-all, approach to contemplation and meditation. It provides a method for gaining deep *insight* and direct experience into the nature and purpose of our lives.

INTEGRATION

Taken together, these two processes help us to develop a solid and sustainable inner foundation for the *integration* of our deepest insights and values into the world. The Mandala and ISM provide a process for "leading from within." This is not always easy, but if we gradually and gently engage in the process, over the long-term it will bear fruit.

THE BOOK, WORKBOOK & WEBSITE

This workbook is a companion to my book, *Mandala: Creating an Authentic Spiritual Path – An InterSpiritual Process.* This book describes a process for creating your spiritual path by discovering, actualizing, and balancing your twelve families of archetypal spiritual styles. Then, through the lenses of these styles you will explore answers to your deepest spiritual questions and discern spiritual practices from among twelve families of spiritual and secular resources.

It is being used for in-person and online classes, for short programs and retreats, and for private mentoring. Its purpose is to help you engage in this process, to develop your own spiritual path and to lead your life towards greater harmony, unified with your deepest spiritual insights and values. This Mandala Process provides a container for cultivating your inner path that will guide you in all aspects of your life. It offers a process, not answers.

Both my book and website share stories about how I came to the Mandala Process and how the recognition of my own spiritual styles and questions has helped me to define my own personal path. Whether you are creating your personal path within a single tradition or from among a variety of traditions and resources, I hope my personal story will illustrate how this process might also work for you.

The Mandala Process described here is an integral component in a larger process of insight and integration. It is accompanied by a contemplative process called "InterSpiritual Meditation: A Seven-Part Process from the World's Spiritual Traditions." When you engage in "ISM" from the perspective of your spiritual styles and questions, new insights will emerge to help guide your internal spiritual path so that you might actively participate in the world by "leading from within."

This workbook is designed to be used in classes, retreats, and personal mentoring. However, its contents are also available on a website that has been especially created to support the Mandala Process process. The website is the foundation for online courses, as it contains the Spiritual Paths Profiling Instrument. It also provides excerpts from my book and links to related online materials, as well as allowing for discussions between students and the teacher.

This workbook has five parts:
Part 1: An introduction and overview of the Mandala Process Process.
Part 2: The Spiritual Paths Profiling Instrument™.
Part 3: Exercises for gaining clarity and harnessing your archetypal spiritual styles.
Part 4: The Spiritual Questions Profiling Instrument™.
Part 5: Exercises to help you find answers to your questions through the lenses of your archetypal spiritual styles.

DEFINITIONS

Spirituality I take to be concerned with those qualities of the human spirit
— such as love and compassion, patience, tolerance, forgiveness,
contentment, a sense of responsibility, a sense of harmony
which bring happiness to both self and others.
— His Holiness the Dalai Lama

Words like "religion," "spirituality," and "archetype" are loaded with various meanings and associations depending on one's school of thought or personal bias. Therefore, at the outset I am defining my terms, in order that we may share a vocabulary.

Religion:
> from the Latin, religio, meaning, "to reconnect, to bind together or link back."

Spirit:
> from the Latin, spiritus, meaning, "breath, soul, life, essence."

Spiritual:
> from the Latin spiritualis meaning "of the spirit," pertaining to "the essence" of life

InterSpiritual:
> the shared processes, insights, intentions, and experiences found among people of all traditions leading to spiritual knowledge and integrity.

Archetype:
> a universally understood symbol, term, or pattern of behavior; a prototype upon which others are copied, patterned, or emulated.

Style:
> a mental (cognitive, emotional, behavioral) predisposition; a distinctive way of perceiving, processing, and expressing information.

STYLES, WAYS, TYPES & ARCHETYPES

We are using the term "style" to connote your natural way of learning and expressing yourself. For example, your learning style might be musical, mathematical, kinesthetic, artistic, or interpersonal. Your style provides a kind of lens through which you take in, interpret, and act on information. In this work, I am suggesting twelve families of spiritual styles through which you process and put into practice knowledge pertaining to spirituality. There are a variety of opinions about where your styles come from. Some hypothesize that your style might be physically "hardwired" into your brain. Others hold they might be developed by social conditioning. Still others maintain that they might come from your *karma*, soul, God, or from some type of universal consciousness. For me, the question of how and why they exist is simply a delicious mystery.

To describe the styles, we are also going to be using terminology like "Way of the Arts," "Way of the Body," and so on. This is just another way to name our inner spiritual predispositions, predilections, or styles. These styles might also be called "types." However, this term is often used to describe distinctive personalities and behavioral styles as in such type systems as Myers-Briggs or the Enneagram. Although there are similarities, I am trying to avoid confusion that might come from using the same terminology.

We are using the term "archetypal spiritual style," meaning a universally shared pattern of behavior; or a personality type, style, or way of being expressed in human beings everywhere. For many, the term "archetype" implies the existence of an underlying universal consciousness or ground-of-being from which these archetypes emerge. While there are compelling arguments in favor of this view, my use of the term archetype is not wedded to this assumption.

However they exist, these archetypal spiritual styles are somehow embedded in the recesses of your consciousness and they influence your attitudes, your ways of learning, your choice of spiritual beliefs, and practices. Knowingly or unknowingly, you are predisposed by these internal propensities for spiritual learning and practice. The harnessing and balancing of these primary archetypes, while not sufficient alone for cultivating our spiritual path, is a necessary condition for accessing the wisdom nascent within you, and accessing the riches within the world's spiritual, mythological, psychological, indigenous and scientific resources. When you honor and cultivate the unique attributes of each style, you are well equipped to actualize the fullness of your human and spiritual potential.

OVERVIEW OF THE MANDALA PROCESS

Before we begin to define and work with your individual spiritual style profiles, please review a brief summary of how the Mandala provides a general container for the individual baskets wherein you will store your knowledge and practices leading to your personal path. There are three categories of these baskets. The outer circle illustrates twelve families of spiritual archetypes or styles through which you search for answers and develop your paths. The middle circle illustrates twelve families of spiritual questions for which you seek answers. The inner circle illustrates twelve families of traditions and resources in which your answers may be found. The white space in the center illustrates your own personal inner path that is the sum total of the knowledge and practices you have collected in each of these twelve baskets. The following line drawing illustrates these three sets of twelve families. As you work with this process, you will create journal entries around each of these categories. Your personal journals will provide the foundation for the creation and refinement of your own paths.

THE MANDALA PROCESS

TWELVE FAMILIES OF SPIRITUAL STYLES, QUESTIONS AND RESOURCES

Twelve Families of Spiritual Styles, Questions & Resources

THE FOLLOWING CHART lists each of these three sets of twelve families of archetypal styles, questions, and resources. These are listed below. But, in your individual Mandala discernment process, you will line up your personal styles with your personal questions and the resource(s) within which you seek answers. This will help you to better focus on your journey of discovery.

	Archetypal Styles	Questions	Resources
1	Arts (The Artist)	Consciousness	Buddhism
2	Body (The Mover)	Death	Christianity
3	Contemplation & Meditation (The Contemplative)	Existence	Hinduism
4	Devotion (The Devotee)	Freedom	Islam
5	Imagination (The Dreamer)	God	Judaism
6	Love (The Lover)	Good & Evil	Taoism
7	Mystic (The Mystic)	Happiness	The 12 Steps of AA
8	Nature (The Naturalist)	Reality	Indigenous, Shamanic
9	Prayer (The Prayer)	Soul	Other
10	Reason (The Thinker)	Spirit Beings	Psychology, Philosophy, Mythology
11	Relationships (The Mensch)	Suffering	Science
12	Wisdom (The Sage)	Transformation & Ultimate Potential	Spiritual But Not Religious (SBNR)

THE ARCHETYPAL STYLES

For brevity, each of these twelve families of archetypal styles is listed by a single word. But they should be read as "The Way of the Arts," "The Way of the Body," and so on. Further, each of these twelve connotes a broader family of spiritual archetypes. For example, "The Path of Devotion" connotes a family of related styles like faith, belief, and ritual. The purpose of this list of twelve is not to be comprehensive, but to be inclusive. They are meant to prompt you to ask yourself such questions as: "How do I learn," "What is my spiritual archetype," and "What is my spiritual style?" During the course of your life, your primary and contributing archetypes will change. Each is like a tributary flowing into the river of your life, or branches of trails that eventually will join into a single life-path.

THE QUESTIONS

The single word for each of the twelve spiritual questions connotes a family of related questions. These are the grand questions we begin asking as children. They are the perennial, universal questions that have been asked by scientists, philosophers, and theologians throughout the ages. For example, the question of consciousness connotes questions like: "What is mind?" "How do I know?" "Is consciousness produced by the brain?" "What is the ultimate potential of consciousness?" "Does my consciousness survive bodily death?" These questions are meant to inspire you to ask your own questions and embrace the mysteries that await your discovery as you define your own spiritual path.

THE RESOURCES

This process for discerning your own archetypal style, honoring your own questions, and finding your own answers, can be utilized within a single spiritual resource or among a variety of resources. Whether your path is formed within a single or multiple resources, this Mandala process is designed to help you engage in a life-long adventure of exploration and discovery leading to the development of your own personal path.

Engaging & Balancing Your Spiritual Styles

In the following pages, there is a summary of these "12 families of spiritual styles" and the "12 families of spiritual questions." I use the words "families of…" because each style and question can open up into a number of other closely related styles that might seem more appropriate for you. The names of these styles and questions are not set in concrete. Rather, they are meant to evoke in you an intuitive realization of your own primary styles and questions. Once this happens, you are ready to begin your personal journey.

Since you embody all twelve styles, to a greater or lesser degree, and since your dominant styles may shift over time, it is important that you recognize, honor, and harness all these spiritual styles within you. It is also important that you realize that one style alone may not be sufficient for the creation of a fully developed spiritual path. For example: your Way of the Mystic might need the support of your Way of Reason. Your Way of the Body might need the support of the Way of Nature. Your Way of Meditation might need the support of Prayer. Your Way of Relationships might need the support of your Way of Love and Compassion. Once all your archetypal spiritual styles are working together harmoniously, your personal spiritual path can become mature, satisfying, and sustainable. There will be no internal conflicts to impair your progress.

Our work together should also be supported by your own independent research on spiritual styles and questions. Remember, the Mandala provides a process, not answers. It will be up to you to move through each of the twelve families of styles, questions, and resources as an outline to be filled in through your own research, experimentation and discernment. Working independently, as well as with your mentors and companions, you can begin to find the answers and practices that will define your spiritual path. Here are some of the learning resources to consider.

- ☐ Teachers, mentors, and authors whose styles of learning and teaching match your own.
- ☐ Spiritual resources and practices developed by and for people with your spiritual styles that can help you find answers to your questions.
- ☐ Books and classes on learning styles, personality types, and universal archetypes.
- ☐ Stories of mythological and historical figures whose archetypes match yours and whose challenges give you greater insight into your own predispositions.
- ☐ Activities, resources, and practices that engage your less dominant archetypal styles that will support and balance your primary styles and fill in the gaps in your overall spiritual development

☐ The Internet, which provides an amazing resource for your journey, so long as you are focused on your specific styles and questions. Without this focus, it is easy to get lost and sidetracked by a dizzying array of possibilities.

I cannot overstate the importance of keeping a detailed journal during the entirety of this process. Your journal can be divided into the categories of both the Mandala Process and InterSpiritual Meditation. Your journal will provide the baskets into which you will store the knowledge, methods, and experiences you are gaining along the way. It will provide a comprehensive record of your spiritual journey. Eventually your journal will provide a fully developed picture of your personal spiritual path and it will help guide you throughout all the stages of your life.

Because the space for journaling is limited in this workbook, you might want to acquire a multipage journal or notebook and divide it into sections for each of the spiritual styles and questions. This will provide you with additional space so that you can continue this process over time. As you do this, you will discover how your spiritual insights evolve and deepen over time. When you integrate this process with the seven-step process of InterSpiritual Meditation, your journal will provide an outline and content of your personal contemplative practice. In this way, your journal(s) will define your personal spiritual path and even convey your spiritual legacy to your loved ones.

THE 12 FAMILIES OF SPIRITUAL STYLES

A BRIEF SUMMARY

Here are brief summaries of the twelve spiritual styles and questions.

1. "The Artist" — The Way of the Arts

The Artist finds spiritual inspiration, beauty, as well as personal expression through painting, drawing, sculpture, music, dance, and poetry.

2. "The Kinesthete" — The Way of the Body

The Kinesthete uses physical movement as a primary mode of learning and somatically experiences subtle emotional and spiritual states of consciousness in various parts of their body.

3. "The Meditator" — The Way of Contemplation and Meditation

The Meditator and Contemplative are drawn to quiet and solitary introspection and seeks to discover the truth within or through communion with the numinous.

4. "The Devotee" — The Way of Devotion

The Devotee is naturally loyal and committed to a job, relationship, a set of principles, a way of life, a ritual daily routine, a religious teacher, a spiritual tradition, or a life goal.

5. "The Dreamer" — The Way of Imagination

The Dreamer naturally dwells in the imaginary awareness of the possibilities of being and intrigued by images arising from the limitless depths of consciousness.

6. "The Lover" — The Way of Love and Compassion

The Lover naturally experiences the universality of love and seeks to bring happiness and to relieve the suffering of others.

7. "The Mystic" — The Way of the Mystic

The Mystic naturally feels, intuits, communes with, or otherwise experiences mysteries of the numinous that lie beyond the boundaries of ordinary human perception.

8. "The Naturalist" — The Way of Nature

The Naturalist is most at ease when absorbed into the forests, deserts, plains, mountains, streams, and oceans of the natural environment, in harmony with shared elements of existence.

9. "The Prayer" — The Way of Prayer

The Prayer naturally seeks the guidance, help, strength, healing, or forgiveness from a sacred being or divine source whose capabilities supersede those of ordinary human beings.

10. "The Thinker" — The Way of Reason

The Thinker needs to figure things out and to create a reasonable foundation for all aspects of spiritual practice.

11. "The Mensch" — The Way of Relationships

The Mensch naturally learns, expresses, and creates a spiritual path through compassionate interaction in community with others.

12. "The Sage" — The Way of Wisdom

The Sage embodies the wisdom of a long life fully-lived and the realization of truths transmitted by profound wisdom holders throughout the ages.

THE 12 FAMILIES OF SPIRITUAL STYLES
QUESTIONS

1. Consciousness

What is consciousness? What is its potential? Is my consciousness confined to my brain and nervous system? Is my personal conscious connected to a universal sphere of consciousness?

2. Death

What happens to my consciousness when my body dies? How can death be an integral part of my spiritual practice?

3. Existence

Is there a beginning or end to existence? Did life evolve from atomic particles and energy, or was it created by a pre-existing God or divine force? What is the relationship between consciousness and existence?

4. Freedom

Is it possible to be free from the struggles of normal life? What would total freedom from struggles look like? How can I experience more freedom?

5. God

What is God? Is there a universal creator or divine creative energy behind all that exists?

6. Good & Evil

What is "the good?" Must I be wise to be good? Do I need to be good to be happy? What does it mean to be a good person? Why do bad things happen to good people? If God is all loving, is there another source of evil in the universe?

7. Happiness

Is happiness the same as fun and enjoyment? What is true happiness, how do I achieve it?

8. Reality

Does the world around me exist in the way I perceive it? How much of the external world is created by my own bias and projection? Is reality relative to the perceiver?

9. Soul

Do I have a soul that is independent, eternal, and permanent? Is there a real "me" that exists behind all of my thoughts, experiences, emotions, and perceptions? Do I have free will or am I under the control of other forces? Am I created by God? Am I just my physical mind and body that will die when my body dies?

10. Spirit Beings

Are there other intelligent, non-earthly beings with whom I can communicate? Just because there are spirit beings, can I believe and trust what they have to say?

11. Suffering

Why do I suffer? What is the cause of my suffering? How can I heal the causes of my suffering?

12. Transformation & Ultimate Potential

Are there limits to my personal potential for mental, spiritual, and physical evolution? What is the grandest possibility for my existence? Do I have the capacity to transform myself into my ideal being? How should I engage in my own transformation?

INQUIRY, INSIGHT & INTEGRATION

The overall Spiritual Paths Process is summarized by three words: inquiry, insight, and integration. This workbook on the Mandala Process pertains primarily to the part of your journey called "Inquiry." In part two of your journey, the section entitled, "Insight," you will explore and create a personally meaningful contemplative practice through the seven-step process of InterSpiritual Meditation (ISM). Here, you cultivate a contemplative practice that accompanies and amplifies the capacities of your other archetypal spiritual styles. In part three of your journey, that which I'm calling "Integration," you engage in the world supported by the wisdom and practices engaged in parts one and two. This is not a linear but an integral process for all three weave in and out of each other throughout the course of your life.

The full process of InterSpiritual Meditation (ISM) is covered in my book, workbook, and the online course. It is the subject of periodic retreats and classes and personal mentoring. A summary of this meditation is included at the end of this workbook.

INQUIRY
Discovering Your Personal Path

The Mandala

Honoring your Spiritual Styles
& Questions

INSIGHT
Creating Your Contemplative Practice

InterSpiritual Meditation

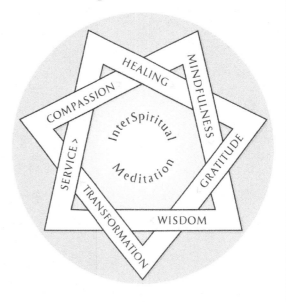

Seven-Step Process
A Foundation for Action & Service

INTEGRATION
Engaging Life with Equanimity, Wisdom & Compassion

Business	Environment	Peace-Making
Career	Family	Play
Community	Healthcare	Political Action
Education	Law Enforcement/Military	Psychology
End-of-Life	Ministry	Relationships
		Social Justice/Activism

PART TWO

SPIRITUAL STYLES — A PROFILE INSTRUMENT

Spiritual Styles - Profile Instrument

Instructions

PART TWO OF THIS workbook contains a three-step process to help you discern your spiritual styles at this juncture of your life. If you are also taking this course through the website, this profile instrument is also available online in a more automated form. It is provided here in paper form for use in learning settings where online connectivity is not possible.

The instrument will help you discover your archetypal spiritual styles, use them to find your spiritual answers and create your spiritual path.[1] These styles may shift over the course of your life. Therefore, the present results of this survey are informative but not fixed for all time. This instrument can be retaken from time to time to see how your primary styles shift. Doing so will help you to adjust your spiritual learning and practices accordingly.

This instrument has four parts:

Step 1: Ranking Your Spiritual Preferences using the Spiritual Styles Profile Tool
Step 2: Calculating Your Spiritual Preferences
Step 3: Summarizing of Your Preferences
Step 4: Coloring in Your Own Personal Spiritual Styles Mandala

---

1 I would like to thank Dr. Carol S. Pearson for her books and related workbooks, *Awakening the Hero Within*. Her works and advice helped formulate the Spiritual Styles Instrument.

SPIRITUAL STYLES — PROFILE INSTRUMENT
STEP 1: RANKING YOUR SPIRITUAL PREFERENCES

DATE: _____   NAME: _____

Please read the following questions and give yourself a numerical rating indicating your level of resonance with these statements. 1=Never, 2=Rarely, 3=Occasionally, 4=Often, 5=Always.

1	I am naturally comfortable with creative or artistic expression.	
2	I naturally feel my emotional states through areas in my physical body.	
3	I like silence, without distraction to observe the inner workings of my mind.	
4	I naturally tend to be devoted to a job, person, ideology, or community.	
5	I often have vivid and memorable dreams.	
6	I naturally have a kind-hearted feeling toward others.	
7	I am attracted to the possibility of mystical visions and revelations.	
8	I find tranquility in the forests, mountains, deserts, streams, lakes, and oceans.	
9	I am inclined to pray to a God, deity, higher power, or universal consciousness.	
10	I like to ponder the universal questions of existence.	
11	I am naturally inclined to close relationships with family, friends, and colleagues.	
12	I believe it is possible to gain wisdom from a source beyond the senses and intellect.	
13	I am inspired by artistic expressions of a spiritual nature.	
14	I gravitate toward a specific physical activity to foster peace, tranquility, and insight.	
15	I am comfortable spending considerable quiet time alone.	

16	I am more prone to faith than skepticism.	
17	I am drawn to spiritual symbols, icons, and imagery.	
18	My primary life intention to help others achieve their highest ideals.	
19	I have had paranormal experiences beyond ordinary sense perceptions.	
20	I feel that nature is my connection with the sacred.	
21	I have a daily ritual of prayer for help, guidance, or protection of a higher power.	
22	I like to thoroughly consider something before committing myself to it.	
23	I gain profound insights about the nature of life through relationships with others.	
24	I yearn for wisdom of the true nature of reality.	
25	I gain insight and equanimity from looking and listening to artistic works.	
26	I need a physical practice that fosters peace, spiritual presence, and insight.	
27	I like to carefully consider all the angles before committing to a course of action.	
28	I feel that a devotional practice will enhance my spiritual transformation.	
29	I naturally form an image or a vision of my future goals.	
30	I am naturally motivated to help remove suffering in others.	
31	I have had unexplainable experiences of the supernatural.	
32	I feel oneness or inter-being-ness when immersed in the natural world.	
33	I feel that prayer is an essential part of spiritual practice.	
34	I prefer reason over faith.	
35	I like to help others to learn, to solve problems, make decisions, and become happy.	
36	I long for an enlightened wisdom in order to help others.	
37	I am comfortable observing and creating art relating to my spirituality.	
38	I prefer physical movement as a vehicle for spiritual/contemplative practice.	

39	I am called to discover truth through inner contemplation and meditation.	
40	I believe that devotion in a sacred/higher power is required for spiritual realization.	
41	I am naturally interested in mythological stories and archetypal beings.	
42	I have natural empathy and am moved to help others who are suffering.	
43	I feel connection to an unnamable higher power, being, or universal power.	
44	I feel a special spiritual affinity with certain animals or plants.	
45	I believe there are supra-human beings that can hear my prayers and help me.	
46	I am inclined to ask the big "Why" rather than regular "how" questions.	
47	I think that spiritual practice requires love, kindness, and compassion toward others.	
48	I believe that some beings have attained transcendent wisdom of ultimate reality.	
49	I am inspired to express my deepest feelings through music, dance, art, or poetry.	
50	I naturally want to physically express my innermost insights through movement.	
51	I wish to emulate those who achieve realization through meditative solitude.	
52	I yearn to be devoted to a greater cause or higher principle.	
53	I have had a rich and vivid imagination since childhood.	
54	I feel held in a universal love and compassion from a source beyond me.	
55	I am drawn to an unseen mystery that could reveal the ultimate nature of reality.	
56	I regard nature as my church, spiritual source, or religion.	
57	I receive a special peace and tranquility when I pray.	
58	I regard reason as a necessary foundation for a spiritual practice.	
59	I prefer being in the company of others more than solitude.	
60	I have the potential to attain the wisdom of Buddha, Christ, La Tzu, Mohammed, or Moses.	

SPIRITUAL STYLES — PROFILE INSTRUMENT
STEP 2: CALCULATING YOUR SPIRITUAL PREFERENCES

In the table below, please copy and then add up the numerical rankings you gave for each statement in Step 1.

1. Way of the Arts	Rank	2. Way of the Body	Rank
Statement 1		Statement 2	
Statement 13		Statement 14	
Statement 25		Statement 26	
Statement 37		Statement 38	
Statement 49		Statement 50	
Total		Total	

3. Way of Contemplation	Rank	4. Way of Devotion	Rank
Statement 3		Statement 4	
Statement 15		Statement 16	
Statement 27		Statement 28	
Statement 39		Statement 40	
Statement 51		Statement 52	
Total		Total	

5. Way of Imagination	Rank	6. Way of Love	Rank
Statement 5		Statement 6	
Statement 17		Statement 18	
Statement 29		Statement 30	
Statement 41		Statement 42	
Statement 53		Statement 54	
Total		Total	

7. Way of the Mystic	Rank	8. Way of Nature	Rank
Statement 7		Statement 8	
Statement 19		Statement 20	
Statement 31		Statement 32	
Statement 43		Statement 44	
Statement 55		Statement 56	
Total		Total	

9. Way of Prayer	Rank	10. Way of Reason	Rank
Statement 9		Statement 10	
Statement 21		Statement 22	
Statement 33		Statement 34	
Statement 45		Statement 46	
Statement 57		Statement 58	
Total		Total	

11. Way of Relationships	Rank	12. Way of Wisdom	Rank
Statement 11		Statement 12	
Statement 23		Statement 24	
Statement 35		Statement 36	
Statement 47		Statement 48	
Statement 59		Statement 60	
Total		Total	

SPIRITUAL STYLES — PROFILE INSTRUMENT
STEP 3: SUMMARY OF YOUR PREFERENCES

In the table below write the totals for each of the 12 Paths from the table in Step Two.

1. Way of the Arts		2. Way of the Body	
3. Way of Contemplation		4. Way of Devotion	
5. Way of Imagination		6. Way of Love	
7. Way of the Mystic		8. Way of Nature	
9. Way of Prayer		10. Way of Reason	
11. Way of Relationships		12. Way of Wisdom	

SPIRITUAL STYLES — PROFILE TOOL
STEP 4: YOUR PERSONAL SPIRITUAL STYLES MANDALA

In the Mandala on the following page, please use a pencil or marker to shade or color in the numerical value associated with each of your spiritual styles.

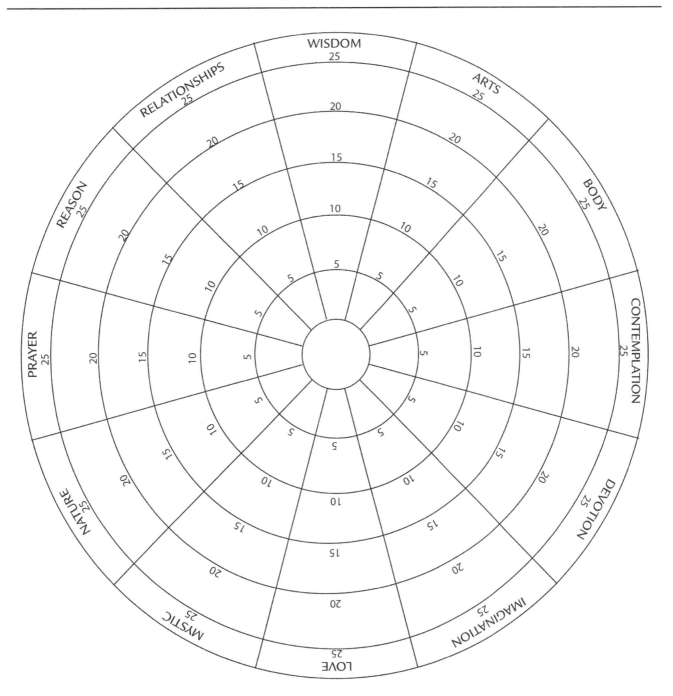

PART THREE

ENGAGING & BALANCING YOUR SPIRITUAL STYLES WORKSHEETS

NOTE: The following worksheets are designed to help you discover and harness your archetypal spiritual styles. The questions prompt you to look into the deep recesses of your mind to uncover the hidden predispositions that shape your way of approaching spiritual answers, practices, and paths. Don't worry if you do not have immediate answers for these questions for they are meant to help you begin the process and then to engage with others in workshops and private mentoring. Once you are aware of your spiritual styles, you can begin to find and develop the best answers and practices for you from within a single tradition, or from among a variety of compatible traditions and resources.

"The Artist"

The Way of the Arts

The Artist within you finds spiritual inspiration, beauty,
as well as personal expression through painting, drawing,
sculpture, music, dance, or poetry.

Are you naturally comfortable with creative artistic expression?
Are there artists and works of art that give expression to your sense of the spiritual?
Does participating in art, poetry, music, and dance inspire and bring out the spiritual within you?
How will you harness your Way of the Arts to create your spiritual path?

If your answer to these questions is "yes," then the Way of the Arts might be one of your primary styles for spiritual learning and practice. Aesthetic learners express and experience spirituality through creative expression. This is because intellectual concepts and words often fail to capture, for example: an epiphany of the transcendent, the marvelous geometric designs of existence, the mysterious shapes and colors of creation, the sparkling galaxies of universe, the poetry of Rumi, the music of Bach, the dance of Fonteyn, or the paintings of Michelangelo. It is the natural affinity for spiritual aesthetics that inspires the "Asthete" to expand and deepen their inner sense of the sacred and their creation of a spiritual path.

YOUR PERSONAL WORK SHEET

_____ Numerical value of The Way of the Arts on your hierarchy of spiritual styles.

_____ Rank of The Way of the Arts on your present hierarchy of spiritual styles.

What artists, art forms, and pieces evoke, inspire, and activate the sense of the spiritual within you?

What types of art do you create to express the spiritual within and around you?

Are there new art forms and practices you would like to cultivate and teachers that you would like to learn from? If so, name them.

What are the strengths and limitations for you when approaching spiritual knowledge and practice through the arts?

What other spiritual styles could you engage to balance and support your Way of the Arts?

If the Way of the Arts is not your primary style, what can you do to awaken and engage this style in the service of your own spiritual development?

What are your primary questions to be explored and answered through the arts?

_____ Consciousness	_____ God	_____ Soul
_____ Death	_____ Good	_____ Spirit Beings
_____ Existence	_____ Happiness	_____ Transformation
_____ Freedom	_____ Reality	_____ Ultimate Potential

From the perspective of your Way of the Arts, express in your own words your personal questions and list the resources you will use to seek answers. You might also explore how the other archetypal styles within you might support your search for answers.

Continue this exploration in your personal journal.

"THE KINESTHETE"

THE WAY OF THE BODY

*The Kinesthete within you experiences physical movement as a primary
mode of spiritual learning and practice, and somatically experiences
subtle states of consciousness within the body.*

Does your need for physical activity make it difficult to sit still?
Do you like to explore and express your spiritual experiences through movement?
Do you feel subtle and/or profound emotional and spiritual states through your body?
How will you harness your Way of the Body to create your spiritual path?

THE KINESTHETIC STYLE within you finds great pleasure and satisfaction in physical movement and "listening to your body." When a kinesthetic or somatic learner becomes physically inactive, they can loose their emotional balance, lack mental sharpness, suffer from stress, become lazy, lack self-confidence, and become hard to live with.

If your style is the Way of the Body, you might find it difficult to sit still for long periods of meditation, prayer, intellectual study, and ritual. Therefore, you learn and practice spirituality physically, kinesthetically, or somatically. You are drawn to physical labor, gardening, running, yoga, Tai Chi, Chi Gong, breathing practices, running, walking, climbing, cooking and serving meals, etc. You might find that the focus of physical exercise helps you achieve a single-pointed, tranquil, endorphin-driven bliss. You might find that your greatest epiphanies arise when your body is engaged in just the right form of movement.

Your Personal Work Sheet

_____ Numerical value of The Way of the Body.

_____ Rank of The Way of the Body on your present hierarchy of spiritual styles.

What physical teachers, activities, and feelings connect you with the spiritual dimensions of life?

What physical activities do you use to express the spiritual within and around you?

Are there new physical activities and practices you would like to cultivate and teachers that you would like to learn from? If so, name them.

What are the strengths and limitations for you when approaching spiritual knowledge and practice through the body?

What other spiritual styles could you engage to balance and support your Way of the Body?

If the Way of the Body is not your primary style, what can you do to awaken and engage this style in the service of your own spiritual development?

What are your primary questions to be explored and answered through the Way of the Body?

____	Consciousness	____	God	____	Soul
____	Death	____	Good	____	Spirit Beings
____	Existence	____	Happiness	____	Transformation
____	Freedom	____	Reality	____	Ultimate Potential

From the perspective of your Way of the Body, express in your own words, personal questions and list the resources you will use to seek answers. You might also explore how the other archetypal styles within you might support your search for answers.

Continue this exploration in your personal journal.

"THE CONTEMPLATIVE"

THE WAY OF MEDITATION & CONTEMPLATION

*The Contemplative within you is drawn to quiet and solitary
introspection, and seeks to discover the truth within or through
communion with the numinous.*

Do you long for inner tranquility, focus, and insight?
Are you comfortable spending considerable time in quiet solitude?
Are you called to discover truth and meaning through deep introspection?
How will you harness your Way of Contemplation to create your spiritual path?

THE CONTEMPLATIVE ARCHETYPAL style within you enjoys moments, hours or days of solitude and being absorbed in thought, in the natural environment and in your own natural state of being. This style is a manifestation of your consciousness that enjoys observing the world around you, reflecting on the truths revealed through your life experience and the wisdom of great philosophers, scientists and spiritual teachers.

Contemplation and meditation don't have to be practiced while sitting for long periods in silence and solitude. These styles and related disciplines can be engaged whether you are sitting, walking, lying down, listening to music, immersed in nature, or engaged in such physical activity as swimming, cycling, running, *Tai Chi*, *Chi Gong*, and Yoga. From a spiritual perspective, contemplation, and meditation are essential companions to such other spiritual styles as devotion, the arts, prayer, reason, and relationships.

YOUR PERSONAL WORK SHEET

_____ Numerical value of The Way of Meditation & Contemplation.

_____ Rank of The Way of Meditation & Contemplation on your hierarchy of styles.

What teachers and contemplative activities inspire and activate the sense of the spiritual within you?

What forms of contemplation and meditation do you use to experience the spiritual within and around you?

Are there new contemplative practices you would like to cultivate and teachers that you would like to learn from? If so, name them.

What are the strengths and challenges for you when approaching spiritual knowledge and practice through contemplation and meditation?

What other spiritual styles could you engage to balance and support your Way of the Contemplation?

If the Ways of Contemplation and Meditation are not your primary styles, what can you do to awaken and engage this style in the service of your own spiritual development?

What are your primary questions to be explored and answered through contemplation and meditation?"

_____ Consciousness	_____ God	_____ Soul
_____ Death	_____ Good	_____ Spirit Beings
_____ Existence	_____ Happiness	_____ Transformation
_____ Freedom	_____ Reality	_____ Ultimate Potential

From the perspective of your Way of the Contemplation and Meditation, express in your own words, your personal questions and list the resources you will use to seek answers. You might also explore how the other archetypal styles within you might support your search for answers.

Continue this exploration in your personal journal.

"THE DEVOTEE"

THE WAY OF DEVOTION

*The Devotee within you is naturally loyal and committed to a job,
relationship, set of principles, way of life, ritual daily routine, religious
teacher, spiritual tradition or life goal.*

Do you gravitate more towards faith than skepticism?
Are you are naturally loyal, perhaps to a job, person, or community?
Do you yearn to be dedicated to a greater cause or higher principle?
Do you long to be committed to a spiritual teaching, deity, teacher, or higher power?
How will you harness your Way of Devotion to create your spiritual path?

DIFFICULT LIFE GOALS ARE virtually impossible to achieve without commitment, dedication, and devotion. Creating a spiritual path is no exception. Whether the goal lies in the fields of athletics, academics, the arts, society, or spirituality; you need to be devoted to the objective, to your teacher, and even to the founder of the tradition from which your practices have emerged. Why? Because devotion helps you to be steady, consistent, and determined. Simply put, devotion is a very practical spiritual/psychological tool for creating your path.

YOUR PERSONAL WORK SHEET

_____ Numerical value of The Way of Devotion.

_____ Rank of The Way of Devotion on your present hierarchy of spiritual styles.

What teachers, practices, and devotional settings inspire and activate the sense of the spiritual within you?

What devotional practices do you use to experience the spiritual within and around you?

Are there new devotional practices you would like to cultivate and teachers that you would like to learn from? If so, name them.

What are the strengths and limitations for you when developing your path through devotion?

What other spiritual styles could you engage to balance and support your Way of the Devotion?

If the Way of Devotion is not your primary style, what can you do to awaken and engage this style in the service of your own spiritual development?

What are your primary questions to be explored and answered through the Way of Devotion?

_____ Consciousness	_____ God	_____ Soul
_____ Death	_____ Good	_____ Spirit Beings
_____ Existence	_____ Happiness	_____ Transformation
_____ Freedom	_____ Reality	_____ Ultimate Potential

From the perspective of your Way of Devotion, express in your own words your personal questions and list the resources you will use to seek answers. You might also explore how the other archetypal styles within you might support your search for answers.

Continue this exploration in your personal journal.

"THE DREAMER"

THE WAY OF IMAGINATION

*The Dreamer within you naturally dwells in the imaginary awareness
of the possibilities of being, intrigued by images arising from the
limitless depths of consciousness.*

Do you have vivid, lucid, and memorable dreams?
Are you drawn to spiritual symbols, icons, and imagery?
Have you long had a rich and vivid imagination?
Are you naturally interested in mythological stories and beings?
How will you harness your Way of Imagination to create your spiritual path?

EVERYTHING YOU DO, think, and say involves imagination. This is true whether you are awake or asleep. Imagination is a part of every perception and cognition — the food you choose for breakfast, the thoughts you think, the words you speak, the scents you smell, the forms you feel, and the sounds you hear.

Therefore, as you intentionally set off to create your own spiritual path, it is very helpful to examine the archetypal images residing in the background of your minds. You do so by looking through the lenses of your twelve archetypal styles in the Mandala Process. For each of these is associated with your own internal mental image of, say, the artist, the yogi, the meditator, the devotee, the visionary, the lover, the mystic, the naturalist, the intellectual, the mensch, and the sage.

YOUR PERSONAL WORK SHEET

_____ Numerical value of The Way of Imagination.

_____ Rank of The Way of Imagination on your present hierarchy of spiritual styles.

What teachers, resources, or types of images inspire, inform, and activate the sense of the spiritual within you? (These needn't just be visual images.)

What images do you evoke to enliven the spiritual within and around you?

Are there new imaginal practices you would like to cultivate and teachers that you would like to learn from? If so, name them.

What other spiritual styles could you engage to balance and support your Way of Imagination?

What are the strengths and limitations for you when approaching spiritual practice through imagination?

If the Way of Imagination is not your primary style, what can you do to awaken and engage this style in the service of your own spiritual development?

What are your primary questions to be explored and answered through the Way of Imagination?

_____ Consciousness	_____ God	_____ Soul
_____ Death	_____ Good	_____ Spirit Beings
_____ Existence	_____ Happiness	_____ Transformation
_____ Freedom	_____ Reality	_____ Ultimate Potential

From the perspective of your Way of Imagination, express in your own words, your personal questions and list the resources you will use to seek answers. You might also explore how the other archetypal styles within you might support your search for answers.

Continue this exploration in your personal journal.

"THE LOVER"

THE WAY OF LOVE & COMPASSION

*The Lover within you naturally experiences the universality of love,
seeks to bring happiness, and to relieve the suffering of others.*

Do you have natural, spontaneous empathy for others?
Do you long to serve as a steward of happiness and eliminate suffering?
Do kind-hearted feelings toward others naturally arise in you?
Do you feel embraced by a universal love and compassion greater than you?
How will you harness your Way of Love & Compassion to create your spiritual path?

LOVE IS PERHAPS the most profound, wondrous, and complex word in the human language. Its varied meanings range from intense liking or desire, to the experience of universal interconnectedness and unconditional empathy with the whole of existence. Love and compassion are at the heart of the world's great spiritual traditions. Love is often said to be synonymous with the divine essence of existence and wellspring of all life or whatever name each religion gives to its highest truth.

The Way of Love and Compassion leads you naturally and unquestionably into the service of others. It is the foundation for spiritual activism or engaged spirituality. When your motivation is love, then you compassionately engage with everyone in your families, communities, and professional lives. Your life becomes a living example of your highest ideals, irrespective of your occupation, wealth, or social status. Through this altruistic spiritual love, your empathetic engagement with others becomes the insurance policy for your own personal happiness and wellbeing.

YOUR PERSONAL WORK SHEET

_____ Numerical value of The Ways of Love & Compassion.

_____ Rank of The Ways of Love and Compassion on your hierarchy of spiritual styles.

How does your love and compassion enliven the spiritual within you?

What practices or expressions of love and compassion do you use to experience and extend the spiritual within and around you?

What experiences, people, and resources most influence your practice of love and compassion?

Are there new experiences, expressions, and practices of love and compassion that you would like to cultivate and teachers that you would like to learn from? If so, name them.

What are the strengths and challenges for you when approaching spiritual knowledge and practice through love and compassion?

What other spiritual styles could you engage to balance and support your Way of Love & Compassion?

If the Ways of Love and Compassion are not your primary styles, what can you do to awaken and engage this style in the service of your own spiritual development?

What are your primary questions to be explored and answered through the Way of Love and Compassion?

_____ Consciousness	_____ God	_____ Soul
_____ Death	_____ Good	_____ Spirit Beings
_____ Existence	_____ Happiness	_____ Transformation
_____ Freedom	_____ Reality	_____ Ultimate Potential

From the perspective of your Way of Love and Compassion, express in your own words your personal questions, and list the resources you will use to seek answers. You might also explore how the other archetypal styles within you might support your search for answers.

Continue this exploration in your personal journal.

"The Mystic"

The Way of the Mystic

The Mystic within you naturally feels, intuits, communes with, or otherwise experiences mysteries of the numinous beyond the boundaries of ordinary human perception.

Have you had unexplainable experiences with the supernatural?
Are you attracted to the possibility of mystical visions and revelations?
Have you had paranormal experiences not mediated by your five senses?
Are you drawn to an unseen mystery that could reveal the ultimate nature of reality?
How will you harness your Way of the Mystic to create your spiritual path?

THERE IS A REMARKABLE similarity between the diverse spiritual writing of mystics from many of the world's major religions. Remove the names of their deities and you would think they are members of the same tradition. I use the word "mysteries" because the things a "mystic" perceives are things that can only be wondered about, guessed at, or deduced. They cannot be tangibly perceived or shared through the normal senses of seeing, touching, tasting, smelling, or hearing Mystical perception is one of the ways people approach their spirituality.

YOUR PERSONAL WORK SHEET

_____ Numerical value of The Way of the Mystic.

_____ Rank of The Way of the Mystic on your present hierarchy of spiritual styles.

What types of mystical teachers, experiences, and resources have informed your sense of the spiritual within you?

Are there new mystical experiences and practices you would like to cultivate and teachers that you would like to learn from? If so, name them.

What are the strengths and challenges for you when approaching spiritual knowledge and practice through mysticism?

What other spiritual styles could you engage to balance your Way of the Mystic?

If the Way of the Mystic is not your primary style, what can you do to awaken and engage this style in the service of your own spiritual development?

What are your primary questions to be explored and answered through the Way of Mysticism?

_____ Consciousness	_____ God	_____ Soul
_____ Death	_____ Good	_____ Spirit Beings
_____ Existence	_____ Happiness	_____ Transformation
_____ Freedom	_____ Reality	_____ Ultimate Potential

From the perspective of your Way of the Mystic, express in your own words your personal questions, and list the resources you will use to seek answers. You might also explore how the other archetypal styles within you might support your search for answers.

Continue this exploration in your personal journal.

"THE NATURALIST"

THE WAY OF NATURE

*The Naturalist within you is most at ease when absorbed into the
forests, deserts, plains, mountains, streams, and oceans of the natural
environment, in harmony with shared elements of existence.*

Is nature your gateway to a connection with the sacred?
Do you regard nature your church, religion, or mode of spirituality?
Do you feel a special affinity with certain animals or plants?
Do you feel tranquility, oneness, or inter-being-ness when immersed in nature?
How will you harness the Way of Nature to create your spiritual path?

THE WAY OF NATURE within you is evoked when you immerse yourself in nature and allow your mind to cease its incessant thoughts, emotions, desires, and memories — when you allow yourself to breath gently in and out — when you become absorbed in the shared elements of your existence — when you empty out your false sense of superiority and separation — when you let down your self-imposed boundaries. It is then that you begin to directly intuit and embody your sameness, your unity, your oneness, your interdependence, your reciprocity, and your inter-being-ness.

Sitting by a stream, you integrate yourself into the flow of its waters. You commingle with the plants that are the source of your life-giving breath. You dance in the wind with the butterflies that have recently been transformed from caterpillars. You sing with the birds, you howl with the wolves, you warm yourself by a campfire. When you allow yourself to simply rest and sink deeply into the mystery of your shared existence, you begin to touch the essence of your interconnectedness — the creative force that is beyond your ability to conceive or to name. Through this, you experience unity in diversity.

YOUR PERSONAL WORK SHEET

_____ Numerical value of The Way of Nature.

_____ Rank of The Way of Nature on your present hierarchy of spiritual styles.

In what way does your experience in nature enliven the sense of the spiritual within you?

What experiences, resources, teachers, and activities in nature enable you to experience the spiritual within and around you?

Are there new experiences and practices in nature that you would like to cultivate and teachers that you would like to learn from? If so, name them.

What are the strengths and challenges for you when approaching spiritual knowledge and practice through nature?

What other spiritual styles could you engage to balance your Way of Nature?

If the Way of Nature is not your primary style, what can you do to awaken and engage this style in the service of your own spiritual development?

What are your primary questions to be explored and answered through the Way of Nature?

_____ Consciousness	_____ God	_____ Soul
_____ Death	_____ Good	_____ Spirit Beings
_____ Existence	_____ Happiness	_____ Transformation
_____ Freedom	_____ Reality	_____ Ultimate Potential

From the perspective of your Way of Nature, express in your own words your personal questions, and list the resources you will use to seek answers. You might also explore how the other archetypal styles within you might support your search for answers.

Continue this exploration in your personal journal.

"The Prayer"

The Way of Prayer

The Prayer within you naturally seeks the wisdom, guidance, help, strength, healing, or forgiveness from a sacred being or divine source whose capabilities supersede those of ordinary human beings.

Do you experience peace and tranquility when you pray?
Do you feel that prayer is an essential part of spiritual practice?
Do you have a daily prayer for help, guidance, or protection of a higher power?
Do you believe that there are supra-human beings that hear your prayers and aid you?
How will you harness the Way of Prayer to create your spiritual path?

WHY DO WE PRAY? Many of us turn to prayer when we need help with a problem so grave, a situation so complex, an emergency so dire, a relationship so painful, an illness so sever, a pain so excruciating, that we simply cannot solve it ourselves and there is no person to whom we can turn.

Prayer activates an aspect of your consciousness that is different than your normal desires, wishes, or hopes. For it engages the whole of your being. You put your whole self into prayer — all of your energy and your total focus. You mobilize a force within you that has the capacity to communicate with a transcendent power that can be felt but not seen. Your prayer might come in the form of a song, poem, chant, or dance; it might be accompanied by music, incense, ritual, or tears. It might be transmitted simply in silence, through focus on your breath or meditation on a sacred symbol, word, or truth. It might just be a fervent wish that you float out into the universe.

YOUR PERSONAL WORK SHEET

_____ Numerical value of The Way of Prayer.

_____ Rank of The Way of Prayer on your present hierarchy of spiritual styles.

How does the experience of prayer inspire and activate the sense of the spiritual within you?

What teachers, resources, and types of prayers most enable you to experience the spiritual within and around you?

What are the strengths and challenges for you when approaching spiritual knowledge and practice through prayer?

What other spiritual styles could you engage to balance and support your Way of Prayer?

Are there other modes of praying that you would like to cultivate and teachers that you would like to learn from? If so, name them.

If the Way of Prayer is not your primary style, what can you do to awaken and engage this style in the service of your own spiritual development?

What are your primary questions to be explored and answered through the Way of Prayer?

_____ Consciousness	_____ God	_____ Soul
_____ Death	_____ Good	_____ Spirit Beings
_____ Existence	_____ Happiness	_____ Transformation
_____ Freedom	_____ Reality	_____ Ultimate Potential

From the perspective of your Way of Prayer, express in your own words your personal questions, and list the resources you will use to seek answers. You might also explore how the other archetypal styles within you might support your search for answers.

Continue this exploration in your personal journal.

"The Thinker"

The Way of Reason

The Thinker within you needs to figure things out and have a good reason before engaging in a spiritual practice.

Do you need a good reason before you can have faith?
Do you like to ponder the universal questions of existence?
Do you regard reason as a foundation for a spiritual practice?
Do you naturally ask the metaphysical "Why" questions rather than mechanical "How" questions?
How will you harness the Way of Reason to create your spiritual path?

THE THINKER STRIVES to use logical inference and empirical observation as the basis for determining the realities that lie beyond cognitive and sensory perceptions. This archetypal style seeks certainty about a reality that transcends our transient world — a reality that is the foundation for being — a reality that interconnects all phenomena — a reality that gives meaning and purpose to our lives.

The Way of Reason seeks to prove, for example, the existence of an immortal soul, life after death, or the existence God. It seeks a rational basis for meditation, prayer, devotion, ritual, mystical intuition, and social service. The Path of Reason seeks a solid rational foundation for spiritual practice. For with good reasons to back up the other spiritual styles, then it will be possible to pursue a spiritual path with rigor, joy, faith, and consistency.

YOUR PERSONAL WORK SHEET

_____ Numerical value of The Way of Reason.

_____ Rank of The Way of Reason on your present hierarchy of spiritual styles.

How does logical thinking inspire and inform the sense of the spiritual within you?

What teachers, resources, and modes of intellectual activity inspire your Way of Reason and provide a rational explanation for the spiritual within and around you?

Are there other modes and practices of intellectual activity that you would like to cultivate and teachers that you would like to learn from? If so, name them.

What are the strengths and limitations of approaching spiritual knowledge and practice through the intellect?

What other spiritual styles could you engage to balance and support your Way of the Reason?

If the Way of Reason is not your primary style, what can you do to awaken and engage this style in the service of your own spiritual development?

What are your primary questions to be explored and answered through the Way of Reason?

_____ Consciousness	_____ God	_____ Soul
_____ Death	_____ Good	_____ Spirit Beings
_____ Existence	_____ Happiness	_____ Transformation
_____ Freedom	_____ Reality	_____ Ultimate Potential

From the perspective of your Way of Reason, express in your own words your personal questions and list the resources you will use to seek answers. You might also explore how the other archetypal styles within you might support your search for answers.

Continue this exploration in your personal journal.

"The Mensch"

The Way of Relationships

*The Mensch within you most naturally learns and
expresses spirituality; gains deep satisfaction through
compassionate interaction with others.*

Do you gain wisdom primarily through being in relationship with others?
Do you prefer being in the company of others more than being in solitude?
Do you like to help others to learn, solve problems, and increase their happiness?
Do you enjoy being involved in community projects for the welfare of others?
How will you harness the Way of Relationships to create your spiritual path?

RELATIONSHIPS CAN BE a source of joy or sorrow. Through relationships we see reflections of ourselves while also experiencing our shared human condition as reflected in the lives of others. Relationships are the stage and playground for love and hatred, compassion and narcissism, wisdom and ignorance. Relationships are the basis for a life-long ethical experiment — the living laboratory for testing if and how generosity and kindness generate personal happiness, selfishness, greed, or sadness.

It is in relationships that you are able to learn how virtuous and non-virtuous intentions affect your relative states of happiness and wellbeing. By experiencing joy, grief, love, jealousy — and by the dispassionate observation of these — you recognize the intentions that produce lasting happiness and those that produce sorrow. You directly experience the personal effects of spiritual teachings as you try to apply them in your interactions with others. Healing the wounds of a lifetime is the natural avocation for those whose spiritual style is the Way of Relationships.

YOUR PERSONAL WORK SHEET

_____ Numerical value of The Way of Relationships.

_____ Rank of The Way of Relationships on your present hierarchy of spiritual styles.

How do relationships inspire and inform the sense of the spiritual within you?

What types of relationships or ways of relating evoke the spiritual within and around you?

Who are the people and resources that most inspire the Way of Relationships within you?

Are there other types of relational practices that you would like to cultivate and teachers that you would like to learn from? If so, name them.

What are the strengths and challenges of approaching spiritual knowledge and practice through relationships?

What other spiritual styles could you engage to balance and support your Way of the Relationships?

If the Way of Relationships is not your primary style, what can you do to awaken and engage this style in the service of your own spiritual development?

What are your primary questions to be explored and answered through the Way of Relationships?

_____ Consciousness	_____ God	_____ Soul
_____ Death	_____ Good	_____ Spirit Beings
_____ Existence	_____ Happiness	_____ Transformation
_____ Freedom	_____ Reality	_____ Ultimate Potential

From the perspective of your Way of Relationship, express in your own words your personal questions, and list the resources you will use to seek answers. You might also explore how the other archetypal styles within you might support your search for answers.

Continue this exploration in your personal journal.

"The Sage"

The Way of Wisdom

*The Sage within you embodies the transcendent wisdom of a long
life fully-lived and the realization of truths transmitted by profound
wisdom-holders throughout the ages.*

Do you aspire for wisdom to guide your life and help others?
Do you yearn for transcendent insight into the true nature of reality?
Do you actively seek to unlock your potential to achieve the wisdom of the Buddha,
Christ, La Tzu, Black Elk, Ramakrishna, Mohammed, or Moses?
How will you engage your Way of Wisdom to create your spiritual Path?

WISDOM IMPLIES A KNOWING of truths harvested from the totality of one's life experience. It surpasses the knowledge gained only through intellectual conceptualization and empirical observation. It emerges from the synthesis of all our knowledge gained throughout our lives through the combination of physical, emotional, and intellectual sources, infused and informed by perceptions that reach beyond ordinary appearances and mental projections of reality.

Wisdom is often associated with the feminine. In Buddhism, for example, the Sanskrit word for wisdom is *prajna*, which is feminine, whereas the compassionate method for applying wisdom in the world is associated with the masculine. *Sophia*, the Greek word for wisdom, was adapted by Christianity to connote the knowledge of God that comes from a direct relationship with the divine. *Gnosis*, the Greek term for wisdom, has been used to connote a direct mystical insight and spiritual knowledge of the divine. *Chokhmah*, the Hebrew word for wisdom, also associated with the infinite knowledge of God, connotes direct intuitive insight into the essence or truth of existence. Finally, in Taoism, wisdom, *zhihui*, is the quality of mind that is in harmony with the unnamable essence of the universe.

YOUR PERSONAL WORK SHEET

_____ Numerical value of The Way of Wisdom.

_____ Rank of The Way of Wisdom on your hierarchy of spiritual styles.

How does your own intuitive wisdom inform the sense of the spiritual within you?

Who are the people and resources that most inspire the Way of Wisdom within you?

Are there other types of wisdom practices or resources that you would like to cultivate and teachers that you would like to learn from? If so, name them.

What are the strengths and challenges of approaching spiritual practice through the Way of Wisdom?

What other spiritual styles could you engage to actualize your Way of Wisdom?

If the Way of Wisdom is not your primary style, what can you do to awaken and engage this style in the service of your own spiritual development?

What are your primary questions to be explored and answered through the Way of Wisdom?

____ Consciousness	____ God	____ Soul
____ Death	____ Good	____ Spirit Beings
____ Existence	____ Happiness	____ Transformation
____ Freedom	____ Reality	____ Ultimate Potential

From the perspective of your Way of Wisdom, express in your own words your personal questions, and list the resources you will use to seek answers. You might also explore how the other archetypal styles within you might support your search for answers.

Continue this exploration in your personal journal.

PART FOUR

SPIRITUAL QUESTIONS
PROFILE INSTRUMENT

Spiritual Questions — Profile Instrument
Instructions

Welcome to the Spiritual Questions Profile Tool!
The following profiling tool is designed to help re-awaken your big spiritual questions and begin finding the answers and practices that will define your spiritual path. Since your questions will shift over the course of your life, the present results will be informative but not fixed for all time. This profile instrument can be retaken from time to time to see how your primary questions are evolving. This will help you to make periodic adjustments to your process of spiritual inquiry.

Instructions for Using the Spiritual Questions Profile Tool
Please read the following questions and give yourself a numerical rating indicating your level of interest in these questions. 1 = No Interest, 2 = A Little Interest, 3 = Occasional Interest, 4 = Significant Interest, 5 = Major Interest.

Please do not over-think these questions! Just give each a «gut response» by ranking them 1 - 5 in term of your level of interest right now. This is not a test and there are no right or wrong answers. The goal here is simply to remember, honor, and live into the questions that animate you at this stage of your spiritual journey. Once you focus on a question, you will then harness one or more of your spiritual styles to search for the answers and practices that work best for you.

This instrument has four parts:

Step 1: Ranking Your Spiritual Preferences using the Spiritual Styles Profile Tool.

Step 2: Calculating Your Spiritual Preferences

Step 3: Summarizing of Your Preferences

Step 4: Coloring in Your Own Personal Spiritual Styles Mandala

SPIRITUAL PROFILE TOOL
STEP 1: RANKING YOUR SPIRITUAL QUESTIONS

DATE: _____   NAME: _____

Please read the following questions and give yourself a numerical rating indicating your level of interest in these questions. 1 = None, 2 = A Little, 3 = Moderate, 4 = Significant, 5 = Always.

1	What is consciousness?	
2	What is death?	
3	What is existence?	
4	What is freedom?	
5	What is God?	
6	What is the meaning of "Good?"	
7	What is happiness?	
8	What is reality?	
9	What is the soul?	
10	Do spirit beings (angels, fairies, earth spirits, etc.) exist?	
11	What is suffering?	
12	What is my ultimate potential?	
13	Is consciousness physical and therefore dies with the body?	
14	When my body dies, is that the end of my existence?	
15	Is there a beginning and end to existence?	
16	Is true freedom possible?	
17	Does God have gender and personality?	
18	What is meaning and cause of Evil?	
19	Is happiness the same as fun and enjoyment?	
20	Does the external world exist just as I perceive it?	

21	Do I have a soul and is it the real me?	
22	Are there spirit beings with whom I can communicate?	
23	Why do I suffer?	
24	What is my capacity to be transformed?	
25	What is the potential of consciousness?	
26	Is physical death just a natural event in my continued existence?	
27	Did existence begin with God?	
28	How can I be free?	
29	Am I created in the image of God?	
30	Are good and evil mutually dependent?	
31	Is it possible to by happy all the time?	
32	Is reality dependent on my perception of it?	
33	Is my soul created by God?	
34	Are there spirit beings who are messengers of God or benevolent helpers?	
35	What is the cause of suffering?	
36	How can I actualize my highest potential?	
37	Is consciousness universal or singular to each being?	
38	How can I die before I die and live more fully?	
39	Does existence evolve and does it have a purpose?	
40	Do I have free will and freedom of choice?	
41	Does God observe or control my personal life?	
42	How can I be truly good?	
43	How can I become forever happy?	
44	How can I know the true nature of reality?	
45	Is my soul permanent and eternal?	
46	Can I rely on the messages of spirit beings as infallibly true?	
47	Can I eliminate suffering?	
48	Does transformation require eliminating obstacles/acquiring new capacities?	

49	Is consciousness the basis of my existence?	
50	How can death be seen as a gift rather than a threat?	
51	Does the existence of existence depend on my perception of it?	
52	Can there be freedom without bondage?	
53	Is God just a name for the unnamable power and mystery of existence?	
54	Must I be good to be happy?	
55	Is it possible to be happy while relieving the suffering of others?	
56	Must I understand the true nature of reality to become happy and free?	
57	Do I have a soul, or core of my being, that is eternal yet ever changing?	
58	Are spirit beings just subjective projections of my own consciousness?	
59	What is the cure for suffering?	
60	What practices for transformation are right for me?	

SPIRITUAL PROFILE INSTRUMENT
STEP 2: CALCULATING YOUR SPIRITUAL QUESTIONS

In the table below, please copy and then add up the numerical rankings you gave for each statement in Step 1.

1. Consciousness	Rank	2. Death	Rank
Statement 1		Statement 2	
Statement 13		Statement 14	
Statement 25		Statement 26	
Statement 37		Statement 38	
Statement 49		Statement 50	
Total		Total	

3. Existence	Rank	4. Freedom	Rank
Statement 3		Statement 4	
Statement 15		Statement 16	
Statement 27		Statement 28	
Statement 39		Statement 40	
Statement 51		Statement 52	
Total		Total	

5. God	Rank	6. Good & Evil	Rank
Statement 5		Statement 6	
Statement 17		Statement 18	
Statement 29		Statement 30	
Statement 41		Statement 42	
Statement 53		Statement 54	
Total		Total	

7. Happiness	Rank	8. Reality	Rank
Statement 7		Statement 8	
Statement 19		Statement 20	
Statement 31		Statement 32	
Statement 43		Statement 44	
Statement 55		Statement 56	
Total		Total	

9. Soul	Rank	10. Spirit Beings	Rank
Statement 9		Statement 10	
Statement 21		Statement 22	
Statement 33		Statement 34	
Statement 45		Statement 46	
Statement 57		Statement 58	
Total		Total	

11. Suffering	Rank	12. Transformation	Rank
Statement 11		Statement 12	
Statement 23		Statement 24	
Statement 35		Statement 36	
Statement 47		Statement 48	
Statement 59		Statement 60	
Total		Total	

SPIRITUAL PROFILE INSTRUMENT
STEP 3: SUMMARY OF YOUR PREFERENCES

In the table below, write the totals for each of the 12 questions from the table in Step Two.

1. Consciousness		2. Death	
3. Existence		4. Freedom	
5. God		6. Good & Evil	
7. Happiness		8. Reality	
9. Soul		10. Spirit Beings	
11. Suffering		12. Transformation	

SPIRITUAL PROFILE INSTRUMENT
STEP 4: YOUR SPIRITUAL QUESTIONS MANDALA

In the Mandala below, please use a pencil or marker to shade or color in the numerical value associated with each of your spiritual questions.

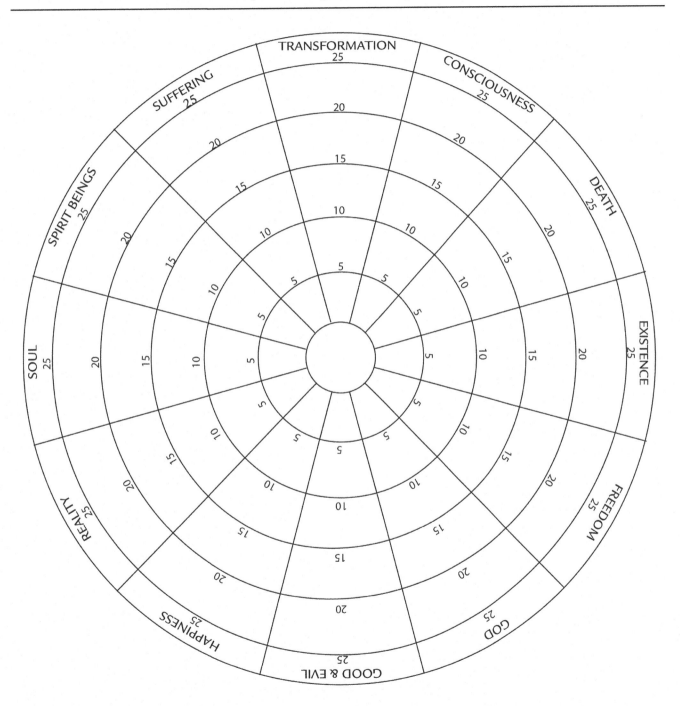

PART FIVE

SPIRITUAL QUESTIONS
EXPLORING ANSWERS
THROUGH THE LENSES OF YOUR
SPIRITUAL STYLES

WORKSHEETS

INTRODUCTION

THERE COMES A TIME in many of our lives when we simply must find our true identity, the meaning and purpose beyond our normal daily activities, our relationships, and our career. This can be a scary time. We may find ourselves knocked out of the trajectory of our pattered life, shaken from the directions that our parents and perhaps even what we feel society laid out for us all while questioning the decisions we have made about how we should live our lives.

This first happened to me in my mid-twenties, so I can empathize deeply with others who have been similarly challenged and blessed. While this can be a difficult time, it is also pregnant with possibilities for a new birth and a new lease on life. The tragedy for many of us, however, is we don't take full advantage of these moments of existential crisis; understandably, for how are we to do this? We might either sink into existential despair or seek the distractions of sensuality, shopping, liquor, drugs, or other forms of distraction. It is not that life's pleasures are evil! It is just that they can distract us from some of life's central issues such as identity, purpose, and meaning. Too often the gifts of "existential crises" remain unopened. Too often, there is nobody and no resource available to us to help us make the most of these grand opportunities.

The possibilities for uncertainty and loneliness always lie in waiting just beneath the surface of our lives. We spend a great deal of our time and money distracting ourselves from the challenges and the opportunities they bring. We build home entertainment systems to still the silence of our inner sanctuaries. We run off to the movies, the bars, the races, and the streets. We have our daily drinks and smokes. We head to the gym and exercise classes. We go shopping for things we want but do not need. We adorn our bodies with make-up, clothing, and tattoos that make us look attractive and confident in our life's direction. We do these things because we think they will make us happy and will quell the existential loneliness that can underlie our lives. And we do them to fend off the questions of identity, meaning, and purpose that await each moment of silence.

During my life, I have discovered that it is the "real men and women" who have the courage to ask the hard questions, to seek meaning and purpose, to develop an inner life, and to live their lives in accordance with universal spiritual values, insights, and goals. This is not easy work, but it is fulfilling beyond all other life pursuits.

Two popular tactics for burying the big questions is to arm ourselves with either skepticism, on the one hand, or blind faith on the other. The skeptic within us might say with great confidence and certainty things like: "There are no ultimate answers." "Searching for answers will just make me miserable." "I don't have time for questions." "These questions have no answers, so why ask." "I've got to compete in this world to make a living and to protect those I love, and these questions just sap my strength and resolve." "Questions are a waste of time . . . I've got a life to lead." "Real men (and women) don't need answers—we just ignore the questions and power-through our doubts and fears."

The diametrically opposed strategy is to ignore the big questions by clinging to blind faith. In this case we leave the questions to 'the professionals,' like priests, rabbis, and scientists, and we just go with the answers they give us. Depending on our religion, we might try to subdue our big questions and force ourselves to believe the answers given by Jesus, Mohammed, the Buddha, Moses, Ramakrishna, Black Elk, Lao Tzu, or Confucius.

These temporary strategies of distraction, skepticism, and blind faith might actually work for a good deal of our lives. But cracks in these defense mechanisms begin to appear when bad things happen to our good friends, to those we love, and to ourselves. They fail in times of silence and boredom. They often fail to comfort us when we near the ends of our own lives. It is in these inevitable moments of existential crisis that we must dig down deep within and reach out to others for answers to the questions that have been with us since childhood. It is then that we must confront the questions we began asking as children and which have lurked in the shadows of our minds ever since.

The solution, it seems to me, is to live our lives into these questions, to accept them, and to embrace the adventures they present. Questions are the energizing juice of life. They provide us with an inner career and a steady drum beat beneath the surface of our professional and personal lives. We can be enlivened by the search and amazed by the marvelous variety of answers that come from great scientists, philosophers, and psychologists, from the lived-wisdom of ordinary people, and from the sages of the world's religions. The answers that we deduce and experience for ourselves become pieces of a puzzle that we gradually assemble to form a coherent picture of our lives and our spiritual paths which guide our active participation in the world.

Since all of us have questions, it is fortunate that there are so many resources for answers within the world's spiritual, philosophical, and scientific resources. There is a wonderful variety of answers --- some contradictory and others complimentary. So, the adventure for us is to engage our primary learning styles and spiritual styles to discover teachers, traditions, and resources to help us discern the answers that make sense to us. Parts Four and Five of this workbook will help us gather our answers through the lenses of our Spiritual Styles.

TWELVE FAMILIES OF SPIRITUAL QUESTIONS

1. Consciousness

What is consciousness? What is its potential? Is my consciousness confined to my brain and nervous system? Is my personal consciousness connected to a universal sphere of consciousness?

2. Death

What happens to my consciousness when my body dies? How can death be an integral part of my spiritual practice?

3. Existence

Is there a beginning or end to existence? Did life evolve from atomic particles and energy, or was it created by a pre-existing God or divine force? What is the relationship between consciousness and existence?

4. Freedom

Is it possible to be free from the struggles of normal life? What would total freedom look like? How can I be free?

5. God

What is God? Is there a universal creator or divine creative energy behind all that exists?

6. Good & Evil

What is "good?" Must I be wise to be good? Do I need to be good to be happy? What does it mean to be a good person? Why do bad things happen to good people? If God is all loving, is there another source of evil in the universe?

7. Happiness

Is happiness the same as fun and enjoyment? What is true happiness, how do we achieve it?

8. Reality

Does the world around me exist in the way I perceive it? How much of the external world is created by my own bias and projection? Is reality relative to the perceiver?

9. Soul

Do I have a soul that is independent, eternal, and permanent? Is there a real "me" that exists behind all of my thoughts, experiences, emotions, and perceptions? Do I have free will or am I under the control of other forces? Am I created by God? Am I just my physical mind and body that will die when my body dies?

10. Spirit Beings

Are there other intelligent, non-earthly beings with whom I can communicate? Just because there are spirit beings, can I believe and trust what they have to say?

11. Suffering

Why do I suffer? What is the cause of my suffering? How can I heal the causes of my suffering?

12. Transformation & Ultimate Potential

Are there limits to my personal potential for mental, spiritual, and physical evolution? What is the grandest possibility for my existence? Do I have the capacity transform myself into my ideal being? How should I engage in my own transformation?

Consciousness

What is consciousness?
Is consciousness the basis of my existence?
What is the potential of my consciousness?
Is consciousness universal or singular to each being?
Is consciousness physical and therefore dies with the body?

IN THIS SECTION, examine your questions related to consciousness from the perspective of one or more of your own spiritual styles:

First, reformulate the question in your own words.

Second, decide which styles you will utilize to explore answers.

Third, write out your present answers and perspectives related to this question.

Fourth, engage in your own exploration from a wide range of resources (internet, books, audio, video, teachers, scriptures, etc.) to discover personally meaningful answers and perspectives.

Fifth, as you begin your daily meditations, gently imbed the question deeply within your consciousness and patiently let it rest there. Over time, without expectation for a quick answer, your natural wisdom can emerge around this question.

Sixth, explore and participate in a variety of spiritual practices to help discern your answer.

Seventh, as your insights emerge around this question, express these in your journal.

Please be patient, settle in, and enjoy the gradual process of exploration and discovery.

YOUR PERSONAL WORK SHEET

_____ Numerical value of The Question of Consciousness.

_____ Rank of The Question of Consciousness on your hierarchy of spiritual questions.

Through which of your spiritual style(s) will you explore possible answers to this question.

____ The Arts	____ Imagination	____ Mystic	____ Reason
____ The Body	____ Love	____ Nature	____ Relationships
____ Devotion	____ Meditation	____ Prayer	____ Wisdom

In your own words, how would you restate this question?

How will you harness your styles to explore the right answers for you?

What teachers, teachings, and resources will you explore in your process of discovery?

What spiritual practices will you engage in to discover your answers?

What is your answer to this question at this stage of your process of exploration?

Continue this exploration in your personal journal.

DEATH

What is death?
How can I "die before I die" and yet live more fully?
When my body dies, is that the end of my existence?
How can death be seen as a gift rather than a threat?
Is death simply an integral part of my life and continued existence?

IN THIS SECTION, examine your questions related to death from the perspective of one or more of your own spiritual styles:

First, reformulate the question in your own words.

Second, decide which styles you will utilize to explore answers.

Third, write out your present answers and perspectives related to this question.

Fourth, engage in your own exploration from a wide range of resources (internet, books, audio, video, teachers, scriptures, etc.) to discover personally meaningful answers and perspectives.

Fifth, as you begin your daily meditations, gently imbed the question deeply within your consciousness and patiently let it rest there. Over time, without expectation for a quick answer, your natural wisdom can emerge around this question.

Sixth, explore and participate in a variety of spiritual practices to help discern your answer.

Seventh, as your insights emerge around this question, express these in your journal.

Please be patient, settle in, and enjoy the gradual process of exploration and discovery.

YOUR PERSONAL WORK SHEET

_____ Numerical value of The Question of Death.

_____ Rank of The Question of Death on your hierarchy of spiritual questions.

Through which of your spiritual style(s) will you explore possible answers to this question.

____ The Arts   ____ Imagination   ____ Mystic   ____ Reason

____ The Body   ____ Love   ____ Nature   ____ Relationships

____ Devotion   ____ Meditation   ____ Prayer   ____ Wisdom

In your own words, how would you restate this question?

How will you harness your styles to explore the right answers for you?

What teachers, teachings, and resources will you explore in your process of discovery?

What spiritual practices will you engage in to discover your answers?

What is your answer to this question at this stage of your process of exploration?

Continue this exploration in your personal journal.

EXISTENCE

What is existence?
Did existence begin with God?
Is there a beginning and end to existence?
Does existence evolve and have a purpose?
Is the existence of existence dependent on our perception of it?

IN THIS SECTION, examine your questions related to existence from the perspective of one or more of your own spiritual styles:

First, reformulate the question in your own words.

Second, decide which styles you will utilize to explore answers.

Third, write out your present answers and perspectives related to this question.

Fourth, engage in your own exploration from a wide range of resources (internet, books, audio, video, teachers, scriptures, etc.) to discover personally meaningful answers and perspectives.

Fifth, as you begin your daily meditations, gently imbed the question deeply within your consciousness and patiently let it rest there. Over time, without expectation for a quick answer, your natural wisdom can emerge around this question.

Sixth, explore and participate in a variety of spiritual practices to help discern your answer.

Seventh, as your insights emerge around this question, express these in your journal.

Please be patient, settle in, and enjoy the gradual process of exploration and discovery.

YOUR PERSONAL WORK SHEET

_____ Numerical value of The Question of Existence.

_____ Rank of The Question of Existence on your hierarchy of spiritual questions.

Through which of your spiritual style(s) will you explore possible answers to this question.

____ The Arts	____ Imagination	____ Mystic	____ Reason
____ The Body	____ Love	____ Nature	____ Relationships
____ Devotion	____ Meditation	____ Prayer	____ Wisdom

In your own words, how would you restate this question?

How will you harness your styles to explore the right answers for you?

What teachers, teachings, and resources will you explore in your process of discovery?

What spiritual practices will you engage in to discover your answers?

What is your answer to this question at this stage of your process of exploration?

Continue this exploration in your personal journal.

FREEDOM

What is freedom?
Is true freedom possible?
How can I be free?
Do I have free will and freedom of choice?
Can there be freedom without bondage?

IN THIS SECTION, examine your questions related to freedom from the perspective of one or more of your own spiritual styles:

First, reformulate the question in your own words.

Second, decide which styles you will utilize to explore answers.

Third, write out your present answers and perspectives related to this question.

Fourth, engage in your own exploration from a wide range of resources (internet, books, audio, video, teachers, scriptures, etc.) to discover personally meaningful answers and perspectives.

Fifth, as you begin your daily meditations, gently imbed the question deeply within your consciousness and patiently let it rest there. Over time, without expectation for a quick answer, your natural wisdom can emerge around this question.

Sixth, explore and participate in a variety of spiritual practices to help discern your answer.

Seventh, as your insights emerge around this question, express these in your journal.

Please be patient, settle in, and enjoy the gradual process of exploration and discovery.

YOUR PERSONAL WORK SHEET

_____ Numerical value of The Question of Freedom.

_____ Rank of The Question of Freedom on your hierarchy of spiritual questions.

Through which of your spiritual style(s) will you explore possible answers to this question.

____ The Arts	____ Imagination	____ Mystic	____ Reason
____ The Body	____ Love	____ Nature	____ Relationships
____ Devotion	____ Meditation	____ Prayer	____ Wisdom

In your own words, how would you restate this question?

How will you harness your styles to explore the right answers for you?

What teachers, teachings and resources will you explore in your process of discovery?

What spiritual practices will you engage in to discover your answers?

What is your answer to this question at this stage of your process of exploration?

Continue this exploration in your personal journal.

GOD

What is God?
Am I created in the image of God?
Does God have a gender and a personality?
Does God see or even control my life?
Is God a name for the unnamable power and mystery of existence?

IN THIS SECTION, examine your questions related to God from the perspective of one or more of your own spiritual styles:

First, reformulate the question in your own words.

Second, decide which styles you will utilize to explore answers.

Third, write out your present answers and perspectives related to this question.

Fourth, engage in your own exploration from a wide range of resources (internet, books, audio, video, teachers, scriptures, etc.) to discover personally meaningful answers and perspectives.

Fifth, as you begin your daily meditations, gently imbed the question deeply within your consciousness and patiently let it rest there. Over time, without expectation for a quick answer, your natural wisdom can emerge around this question.

Sixth, explore and participate in a variety of spiritual practices to help discern your answer.

Seventh, as your insights emerge around this question, express these in your journal.

Please be patient, settle in, and enjoy the gradual process of exploration and discovery.

YOUR PERSONAL WORK SHEET

_____ Numerical value of The Question of God.

_____ Rank of The Question of God on your hierarchy of spiritual questions.

Through which of your spiritual style(s) will you explore possible answers to this question.

____ The Arts	____ Imagination	____ Mystic	____ Reason
____ The Body	____ Love	____ Nature	____ Relationships
____ Devotion	____ Meditation	____ Prayer	____ Wisdom

In your own words, how would you restate this question?

How will you harness your styles to explore the right answers for you?

What teachers, teachings, and resources will you explore in your process of discovery?

What spiritual practices will you engage in to discover your answers?

What is your answer to this question at this stage of your process of exploration?

Continue this exploration in your personal journal.

Good & Evil

What is the meaning of "good?"
What is the meaning of "evil?"
Can good and evil exist, one without the other?
What does it mean to be good?
Must I be good to be eternally happy?

IN THIS SECTION, examine your questions related to good and evil from the perspective of one or more of your own spiritual styles:

First, reformulate the question in your own words.

Second, decide which styles you will utilize to explore answers.

Third, write out your present answers and perspectives related to this question.

Fourth, engage in your own exploration from a wide range of resources (internet, books, audio, video, teachers, scriptures, etc.) to discover personally meaningful answers and perspectives.

Fifth, as you begin your daily meditations, gently imbed the question deeply within your consciousness and patiently let it rest there. Over time, without expectation for a quick answer, your natural wisdom can emerge around this question.

Sixth, explore and participate in a variety of spiritual practices to help discern your answer.

Seventh, as your insights emerge around this question, express these in your journal.

Please be patient, settle in, and enjoy the gradual process of exploration and discovery.

YOUR PERSONAL WORK SHEET

_____ Numerical value of The Question of Good and Evil.

_____ Rank of The Question of Good and Evil on your hierarchy of spiritual questions.

Through which of your spiritual style(s) will you explore possible answers to this question.

____ The Arts	____ Imagination	____ Mystic	____ Reason
____ The Body	____ Love	____ Nature	____ Relationships
____ Devotion	____ Meditation	____ Prayer	____ Wisdom

In your own words, how would you restate this question?

How will you harness your styles to explore the right answers for you?

What teachers, teachings, and resources will you explore in your process of discovery?

What spiritual practices will you engage in to discover your answers?

What is your answer to this question at this stage of your process of exploration?

Continue this exploration in your personal journal.

HAPPINESS

What is happiness?
How can I become happy?
Is it possible to be happy all the time?
Is happiness the same as having fun and enjoyment?
Is it possible to be happy while relieving the suffering of others?

IN THIS SECTION, examine your questions related to happiness from the perspective of one or more of your own spiritual styles:

First, reformulate the question in your own words.

Second, decide which styles you will utilize to explore answers.

Third, write out your present answers and perspectives related to this question.

Fourth, engage in your own exploration from a wide range of resources (internet, books, audio, video, teachers, scriptures, etc.) to discover personally meaningful answers and perspectives.

Fifth, as you begin your daily meditations, gently imbed the question deeply within your consciousness and patiently let it rest there. Over time, without expectation for a quick answer, your natural wisdom can emerge around this question.

Sixth, explore and participate in a variety of spiritual practices to help discern your answer.

Seventh, as your insights emerge around this question, express these in your journal.

Please be patient, settle in, and enjoy the gradual process of exploration and discovery.

YOUR PERSONAL WORK SHEET

_____ Numerical value of The Question of Happiness.

_____ Rank of The Question of Happiness on your hierarchy of spiritual questions.

Through which of your spiritual style(s) will you explore possible answers to this question.

____ The Arts	____ Imagination	____ Mystic	____ Reason
____ The Body	____ Love	____ Nature	____ Relationships
____ Devotion	____ Meditation	____ Prayer	____ Wisdom

In your own words, how would you restate this question?

How will you harness your styles to explore the right answers for you?

What teachers, teachings, and resources will you explore in your process of discovery?

What spiritual practices will you engage in to discover your answers?

What is your answer to this question at this stage of your process of exploration?

Continue this exploration in your personal journal.

REALITY

What is real?
Does the world exist in the way I perceive it?
Is reality dependent on my perception of it?
How can I know the true nature of reality?
Must I know what is real to become happy and free?

IN THIS SECTION, examine your questions related to reality from the perspective of one or more of your own spiritual styles:

First, reformulate the question in your own words.

Second, decide which styles you will utilize to explore answers.

Third, write out your present answers and perspectives related to this question.

Fourth, engage in your own exploration from a wide range of resources (internet, books, audio, video, teachers, scriptures, etc.) to discover personally meaningful answers and perspectives.

Fifth, as you begin your daily meditations, gently imbed the question deeply within your consciousness and patiently let it rest there. Over time, without expectation for a quick answer, your natural wisdom can emerge around this question.

Sixth, explore and participate in a variety of spiritual practices to help discern your answer.

Seventh, as your insights emerge around this question, express these in your journal.

Please be patient, settle in, and enjoy the gradual process of exploration and discovery.

YOUR PERSONAL WORK SHEET

_____ Numerical value of The Question of Reality.

_____ Rank of The Question of Reality on your hierarchy of spiritual questions.

Through which of your spiritual style(s) will you explore possible answers to this question.

____ The Arts	____ Imagination	____ Mystic	____ Reason
____ The Body	____ Love	____ Nature	____ Relationships
____ Devotion	____ Meditation	____ Prayer	____ Wisdom

In your own words, how would you restate this question?

How will you harness your styles to explore the right answers for you?

What teachers, teachings, and resources will you explore in your process of discovery?

What spiritual practices will you engage in to discover your answers?

What is your answer to this question at this stage of your process of exploration?

Continue this exploration in your personal journal.

SOUL

What is the definition of soul?
Is my soul created by God?
Do I have a permanent soul that is the basis of my existence?
Do I have a soul that is the observer and governor of my mind and body?
Is soul the ever-changing consciousness from one life to the next?

IN THIS SECTION, examine your questions related to the soul from the perspective of one or more of your own spiritual styles:

First, reformulate the question in your own words.

Second, decide which styles you will utilize to explore answers.

Third, write out your present answers and perspectives related to this question.

Fourth, engage in your own exploration from a wide range of resources (internet, books, audio, video, teachers, scriptures, etc.) to discover personally meaningful answers and perspectives.

Fifth, as you begin your daily meditations, gently imbed the question deeply within your consciousness and patiently let it rest there. Over time, without expectation for a quick answer, your natural wisdom can emerge around this question.

Sixth, explore and participate in a variety of spiritual practices to help discern your answer.

Seventh, as your insights emerge around this question, express these in your journal.

Please be patient, settle in, and enjoy the gradual process of exploration and discovery.

YOUR PERSONAL WORK SHEET

_____ Numerical value of The Question of Soul.

_____ Rank of The Question of Soul on your hierarchy of spiritual questions.

Through which of your spiritual style(s) will you explore possible answers to this question.

____ The Arts	____ Imagination	____ Mystic	____ Reason
____ The Body	____ Love	____ Nature	____ Relationships
____ Devotion	____ Meditation	____ Prayer	____ Wisdom

In your own words, how would you restate this question?

How will you harness your styles to explore the right answers for you?

What teachers, teachings, and resources will you explore in your process of discovery?

What spiritual practices will you engage in to discover your answers?

What is your answer to this question at this stage of your process of exploration?

Continue this exploration in your personal journal.

SPIRIT BEINGS

Do spirit beings (angels, fairies, earth spirits, etc.) exist?
Can we communicate with spirit beings?
Are some spirit beings the messengers of God or benevolent helpers?
Can we rely on their messages as being infallibly true?
Are spirit beings subjective projections of our own mind?

IN THIS SECTION, examine your questions related to spirit beings from the perspective of one or more of your own spiritual styles:

First, reformulate the question in your own words.

Second, decide which styles you will utilize to explore answers.

Third, write out your present answers and perspectives related to this question.

Fourth, engage in your own exploration from a wide range of resources (internet, books, audio, video, teachers, scriptures, etc.) to discover personally meaningful answers and perspectives.

Fifth, as you begin your daily meditations, gently imbed the question deeply within your consciousness and patiently let it rest there. Over time, without expectation for a quick answer, your natural wisdom can emerge around this question.

Sixth, explore and participate in a variety of spiritual practices to help discern your answer.

Seventh, as your insights emerge around this question, express these in your journal.

Please be patient, settle in, and enjoy the gradual process of exploration and discovery.

YOUR PERSONAL WORK SHEET

_____ Numerical value of The Question of Spirit Beings.

_____ Rank of The Question of Spirit Beings on your hierarchy of spiritual questions.

Through which of your spiritual style(s) will you explore possible answers to this question.

____ The Arts	____ Imagination	____ Mystic	____ Reason
____ The Body	____ Love	____ Nature	____ Relationships
____ Devotion	____ Meditation	____ Prayer	____ Wisdom

In your own words, how would you restate this question?

How will you harness your styles to explore the right answers for you?

What teachers, teachings, and resources will you explore in your process of discovery?

What spiritual practices will you engage in to discover your answers?

What is your answer to this question at this stage of your process of exploration?

Continue this exploration in your personal journal.

SUFFERING

What is suffering?
Why do we suffer?
What is the cause of suffering?
Can we eliminate suffering?
What is the cure for suffering?

IN THIS SECTION, examine your questions related to death from the perspective of one or more of your own spiritual styles:

First, reformulate the question in your own words.

Second, decide which styles you will utilize to explore answers.

Third, write out your present answers and perspectives related to this question.

Fourth, engage in your own exploration from a wide range of resources (internet, books, audio, video, teachers, scriptures, etc.) to discover personally meaningful answers and perspectives.

Fifth, as you begin your daily meditations, gently imbed the question deeply within your consciousness and patiently let it rest there. Over time, without expectation for a quick answer, your natural wisdom can emerge around this question.

Sixth, explore and participate in a variety of spiritual practices to help discern your answer.

Seventh, as your insights emerge around this question, express these in your journal.

Please be patient, settle in, and enjoy the gradual process of exploration and discovery.

YOUR PERSONAL WORK SHEET

_____ Numerical value of The Question of Suffering.

_____ Rank of The Question of Suffering on your hierarchy of spiritual questions.

Through which of your spiritual style(s) will you explore possible answers to this question.

____ The Arts	____ Imagination	____ Mystic	____ Reason
____ The Body	____ Love	____ Nature	____ Relationships
____ Devotion	____ Meditation	____ Prayer	____ Wisdom

In your own words, how would you restate this question?

How will you harness your styles to explore the right answers for you?

What teachers, teachings, and resources will you explore in your process of discovery?

What spiritual practices will you engage in to discover your answers?

What is your answer to this question at this stage of your process of exploration?

Continue this exploration in your personal journal.

Transformation & Ultimate Potential

What is my ultimate potential?
What is my capacity to be transformed?
How can I actualize my highest potential?
What path of transformation is right for me?
Does transformation require eliminating obstacles and/or acquiring new capacities?

In this section, examine your questions related to transformation and ultimate potential from the perspective of one or more of your own spiritual styles:

First, reformulate the question in your own words.

Second, decide which styles you will utilize to explore answers.

Third, write out your present answers and perspectives related to this question.

Fourth, engage in your own exploration from a wide range of resources (internet, books, audio, video, teachers, scriptures, etc.) to discover personally meaningful answers and perspectives.

Fifth, as you begin your daily meditations, gently imbed the question deeply within your consciousness and patiently let it rest there. Over time, without expectation for a quick answer, your natural wisdom can emerge around this question.

Sixth, explore and participate in a variety of spiritual practices to help discern your answer.

Seventh, as your insights emerge around this question, express these in your journal.

Please be patient, settle in, and enjoy the gradual process of exploration and discovery.

YOUR PERSONAL WORK SHEET

_____ Numerical value of The Question of Transformation and Ultimate Potential.

_____ Rank of The Question of Transformation and Ultimate Potential on your hierarchy of spiritual questions.

Through which of your spiritual style(s) will you explore possible answers to this question.

____ The Arts	____ Imagination	____ Mystic	____ Reason
____ The Body	____ Love	____ Nature	____ Relationships
____ Devotion	____ Meditation	____ Prayer	____ Wisdom

In your own words, how would you restate this question?

How will you harness your styles to explore the right answers for you?

What teachers, teachings, and resources will you explore in your process of discovery?

What spiritual practices will you engage in to discover your answers?

What is your answer to this question at this stage of your process of exploration?

Continue this exploration in your personal journal.

INTERSPIRITUAL MEDITATION

A SEVEN-STEP PROCESS
FROM THE
WORLD'S SPIRITUAL TRADITIONS

InterSpiritual Meditation
A Seven-Step Process

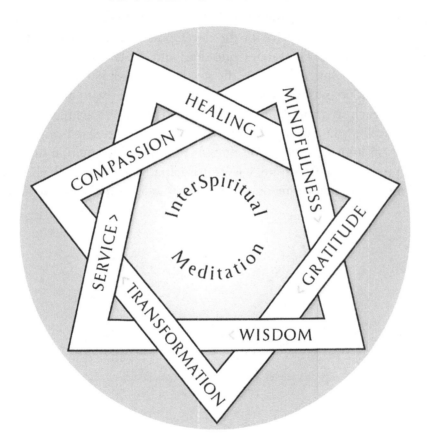

An Integrated Process For
Personal & Group Practice

The Mandala Process helps to provide a foundation for the creation of your personal practice of InterSpiritual Meditation (ISM). ISM provides a structure for the development of personalize meditation practice that suits your unique combination of spiritual styles, questions and experiences. ISM is a personalized process rather than a one-size-fits-all regimen. Each of the seven steps have been drawn from a cross section of the world's major contemplative traditions. Working on your own or with an experience mentor, you can integrate the content into each step based on the wisdom and practice teachings of one or more traditions. Gradually and systematically, you will be able to formulate a personalized practice based on your own unique combination of spiritual styles and questions. For more information on the study and practice of ISM, please refer to my book and website, www.spiritualpaths.net/ISM. Each year, we provide online courses, retreats, and individual mentoring on this process to help you effectively put this into practice.

A Brief Description

THIS CONTEMPLATIVE PROCESS can be shared by people from many diverse perspectives and traditions. It can be practiced alone and in community with others. It pulls together key elements of contemplation and meditation shared by many traditions. In this process we gather in the language of silence and experience inter-connectedness. Joining in stillness, we don't impose on others our own personal beliefs, rituals, or the names for our absolute truths, deities, or God. We honor and celebrate the wise and compassionate practices of all traditions. We discover a profound unity within our diversity. We flourish in the love, peace, compassion, gratitude, and strength of our shared wisdom. We are of one heart. Quietly, each in our own way, we join in the following seven stages together. The sound of a bell leads us from one stage to the next.

1. MOTIVATION: *"May I (We) Be Healthy and Happy"*

Physical, mental, and spiritual health are intertwined; meditation fosters their good health and happiness. We begin meditating with confidence and determination that it will help us heal the innermost causes of illness and suffering. We pray that InterSpiritual consciousness will help heal all beings.

2. GRATITUDE: *"May I (We) Be Grateful for Life's Many Gifts"*

With gratitude, we invoke and honor our teachers, mentors, and great spiritual role models. We invite these great beings to remain present and pray that they guide us. We remind ourselves about the blessings of friends, family, and the environment that nurtures and sustains us.

3. TRANSFORMATION: *"May I (We) Be Transformed Into My Highest Ideal"*

We acknowledge and confess our shortcomings, vowing to patiently persevere in our personal transformation. We vow to remove our inner obstacles and negativities. Without guilt, we forgive others and ourselves as we open to the transformative presence of love.

4. COMPASSION: *"May I (We) Be Loving and Compassionate"*

We set our intention on love and compassion --- the transforming energy for the health and happiness of all. We vow to help all beings be free from the causes of their suffering.

5. MINDFULNESS: *"May I (We) Be Focused and Mindful Through Breathing"*

Mindfully, we concentrate on our breathing. This calms, clears, and focuses our mind. Thoughts, memories, and feelings are observed and released. We focus on our breath, drawing it into the heart-center of our being. Opening ourselves to the reciprocity of universal love, healing, and wisdom we establish the tranquil focus for deep meditation.

6. MEDITATION: *"May I (We) Become Wise Through Meditation"*

Meditation and contemplation are taught in many ways and by many traditions. With sincere respect and appreciation for others, dedicated to our own practice, we silently engage in our own meditation. Alone, or in community, we deepen of our own wisdom as well as our InterSpiritual communion with other diverse experiences of that which we name sacred.

7. DEDICATION: *"May I (We) Serve All Beings with Compassion, Peace, and Wisdom"*

Visualizing our family, friends, colleagues, antagonists, and all beings throughout the world, we rededicate ourselves to becoming stewards of peace, justice and environmental health. May this meditation help us to engage together in the world with patient kindness and wise compassion.

InterSpiritual Meditation
Seven-Step Chart

	Mental State	Prayer	Attributes
1	Motivation	*"May I Be Healthy and Happy."*	Mind Body Spirit
2	Gratitude	*"May I Be Grateful for Life's Many Gifts."*	Remembrance Gratitude Trust Devotion Prayer Offering
3	Transformation	*"May I Be Transformed Into My Highest Ideal."*	Visualizing the Ideal Self-Assessment Confession Remorse Inward Love Forgiveness Surrender Commitment
4	Compassion (Intention)	*"May I Be Loving and Compassionate"*	Exchange Self for Others Reciprocity Universal Love

5	Mindfulness (Attention)	*"May I Be Focused and Mindful Through Breathing."*	Body Position Focus on Breath Concentration & Attention Recollection Patience Perseverance Observation ('Mental Spy') Quiescence
6	Meditation	*"May I Become Wise Through Meditation."*	Tranquil Focus Insight Non-Duality InterBeingness Equanimity Unity Absorption Transcendence Integration
7	Dedication	*"May I Serve All Beings with Compassion, Peace, and Wisdom."*	Visualize applying this in the coming day.

GUIDELINES FOR INTERSPIRITUAL GROUP DISCUSSION

THE PRIMARY LANGUAGE of InterSpiritual dialog is silence. It is the soothing elixir that places each person and each tradition on neutral, reciprocal ground. In silence, we are liberated from our fixed religious or non-religious identities and the words that distinguish one truth from another. We celebrate and welcome the diversity of our respective spiritual styles, traditions, racial, gender, and ethnic diversity. Separately and jointly we experience a wordless quality of the essence of being and the elements of existence that unite us.

When I am liberated by silence, when I am no longer involved in
the measurement of life, but in the living of it, I can discover a
form of prayer in which there is effectively no distraction.
— Thomas Merton

When we enter into conversation with each other, it is important that we maintain this same gentle and kind quality of being. Openness implies vulnerability, therefore we must take great care with our intentions and our words. Opening up to and with each other is rare and delicate occurrence. Therefore, we take great care not to cause another person's shy inner self to recede back into the shadows of his or her consciousness. We create a safe and supportive container within which this contemplative process can unfold. Following are two sets of guidelines to further assist us in aiding and supporting one another.

The first is a list that applies specifically to InterSpiritual dialogues. It is based on ten years of work with contemplative teachers from many traditions with the Spiritual Paths Foundation. The second comes from the work of Parker Palmer that he calls Circles of Trust. Here he provides Touch Stones to guide our conversations and our 'way of being' with each other.

Guidelines Developed in Our Spiritual Paths Programs

• Embrace silence as a common language and the elixir of shared experience and expand your exclusive identity to one that is inclusive and universal.

• Genuinely celebrate and honor the diversity of all spiritual traditions.

• Soften the personal boundaries of fixed identity of your own religion and belief system and open your heart for sincere sharing and learning from the experiences of others.

• Do not respond to a statement by another person with disagreement, agreement, or affirmation. Simply listen compassionately, allowing the statement of another to rest in contemplative reflection and silence.

• Refrain from imposing or projecting your views on others' traditions, beliefs, or practices.

• Refrain from imposing a single universal truth on all religions and spiritual traditions that might not be shared by the traditions themselves.

• If you belong to a specific tradition, speak "from" it rather than "for" it.

• Be careful not to misappropriate, or lift out of context, a specific practice from one tradition and graft it onto another tradition or your practice without knowing its indigenous meaning.

• Engage in contemplative, compassionate listening to draw out wisdom within each participant. Meditatively, observe and release your inner judgments and impulse to react to their words.

PARKER PALMER'S CIRCLES OF TRUST TOUCHSTONES

THE FOLLOWING ARE adapted from Parker Palmer's Touchstones for *Circles of Trust*. More information can be found in his book *A Hidden Wholeness,* or at The Center for Courage and Renewal: www.couragerenewal. org. Palmer's methodology provides an an extremely important grounding for InterSpiritual dialog.

- *Extend and receive welcome.* People learn best in hospitable spaces. In this circle, we support each other's learning by giving and receiving hospitality.

- *Be present as fully as possible.* Be here with your doubts, fears, and failings as well as your convictions, joys, and successes; your listening as well as your speaking.

- *What is offered in the circle is by invitation, not demand.* This is not a "share or die" event! During this time, do whatever your soul calls for, and know that you do it with our support. Your soul knows your needs better than others do.

- *Speak your truth in ways that respect other people's truth.* Your views of reality may differ, but speaking one's truth in a circle of trust does not mean interpreting, correcting, or debating what others say. Speak from your center to the center of the circle, using "I" statements, trusting people to do their own sifting and winnowing.

- *No fixing, no saving, no advising, and no setting each other straight.* This is one of the hardest guidelines for those in the helping professions. But it is one of the most vital rules if you wish to make a space that welcomes soul, the inner teacher.

- *Learn to respond to others with honest, open questions instead of counsel, corrections.* With such questions, you help hear each other into deeper speech.

- *When the going gets rough, turn to wonder.* If you feel judgmental, or defensive, ask yourself, "I wonder what brought her to this belief?" or "I wonder what he's feeling right now?" or "I wonder what my reaction teaches me about myself?" Set aside judgment to listen to others — and to yourself — more deeply.

• *Attend to your own inner teacher.* You learn from others, of course. But as you explore poems, stories, questions, and silence in a circle of trust, you have a special opportunity to learn from within. So pay close attention to your own reactions and responses, to your most important teacher.

• *Trust and learn from the silence.* Silence is a gift in this noisy world, and a way of knowing in itself Treat silence as a member of the group. After someone has spoken, take time to reflect without immediately filling the space with words.

• *Observe deep confidentiality.* Trust comes from knowing that group members honor confidences and take seriously the ethics of privacy and discretion.

• *Know that it is possible to leave the circle with whatever it was that you needed when you arrived.* Know that the seeds planted here can keep growing in the days ahead.

Acknowledgements

There are so many people who have been a part of this endeavor that I wish to thank. I will simply mention their names here without being specific as to why. Sadly, I will have forgotten some significant names that later editions will include. Please forgive me if yours is one of these. My deep gratitude to:

Reverend Gregg Anderson

Rev. Diane Berke

Tessa Bielecki

Bikkhu Bodhi

Reverend Cynthia Bourgeault

Nancy Belle Coe

Katherine and Roger Collis

Father Dave Denny

Lama Palden Drolma

Mollie Favour

Stephanie Glatt

George Haynes

Rabbi Brad Hirschfield

Judy Hyde

Don "Four Arrows" Jacobs

Yogi Nataraja Kallio

Rev. Aaron McEmrys

Sheikh Muhammad Jamal al-Jerrahi (Gregory Blann)

Enrico and Nadia Natali

Susan Pierce

Margot and Tom Pritzker

Jonathan and Diana Rose

Barbara Sargent

Swami Atmarupananda

John Bennett

Robert Bosnak

Robert Bosnak

Mary Ann Brussat

Sister Brahmaprana

Kathy Corcoran

Laura Dixon

Gordon Dveirin

Rob Gabriel

Dr. John Allen Grimes

Sheikha Camille Helminski

Sister Jose Hobday

Pir Zia Inayat-Khan

Reverend Alan Jones

Father Thomas Keating

Reverend Master Khoten

Robert McDermott

Rabbi Leah Novick

Lexie Potamkin

Lynda Rae

Rabbi Jeff Roth

Swami Sarvadevananda

Reverend Lauren Atress

Rabbi Ozer Bergman

Harvey Bottelsen

Joan Borysenko

Loya Cespooch

Ken Cohen

Anita Daniel

Geshe Lobsang Donyo

Suzanne Farver

Gelek Rinpoche

Roshi Joan Halifax

Sheikh Kabir Helminski

James Hughes

Edie Irons

Chief Oren Lyons

Rabbi Miles Krassen

Acharya Judy Lief

Dena Merriam

Brad Miller

Carol Pearson

Reverend Tenzin Priyadarshi

Imam Feisal Abdul Rauf

Sharon Salzburg

Rabbi Zalman Schachter-Shalomi

Rabbi Arthur Gross Schaefer   Dr. Marilyn Schlitz   Christiane Schlumberger
Grace Alvarez Sesma   Rabbi Rami Shapiro   Acharya Judith Simmer-Brown
Ajahn Sona   Geshe Lhundup Sopa   Tina Staley
Michael Stranahan   Tekaronianeken Jake Swamp   Brother Wayne Teasdale
Geshe Lobsang Tenzin   Juliet Spahn-Twomey   Ani Tenzin Kacho
Pravrajika Vrajaprana   Dr. B. Alan Wallace   Radhule Weininger
Sharon Wells   Judy Whetstine   Catherine Wyler
Paula Zurcher

    I am also grateful to all those who have studied InterSpiritual Meditation and the Mandala Process Process with me, for they have helped to clarify and refine the ideas and practices described herein. I am indebted to living examples of my mentors and teachers including Geshe Lhundup Sopa, Father Thomas Keating, Rabbi Zalman Schachter, and His Holiness the Dalai Lama. I am grateful to Zachary Malone, Catherine Wyler who helped edit the first edition of this workbook and Lynda Rae for the initial cover design. I am extremely grateful to Juliet Spohn Twomey and La Casa de Maria for providing encouragement and an incubator for this work. My special thanks also to Carol Pearson for her work and mentorship on formation of the Archetypal Spiritual Styles Profile Instruments. I am deeply grateful to the Aspen Chapel for providing a home for Spiritual Paths Foundation and our board of directors including Jay Hughes, Gregg Anderson, Suzanne Farver, John Bennett, Lexie Potamkin, Mike Stranahan and Harvey Bottlesen. And I am infinitely grateful to my family members, Alexandra and Nulty White, Jonathan Bastian, Paul Keeley, Marianne Bastian and to all my ancestors.

    Finally, I am grateful to Sam Krezinski for layout design and editing, and to Netanel Miles-Yépez for editing and publishing this book.

ABOUT THE AUTHOR

DR. EDWARD W. BASTIAN holds a Ph.D. in Buddhist Studies and is the founder and president of the Spiritual Paths Foundation. His current writing and teaching is the product of over forty years of research and study, especially in the last decades with over fifty esteemed teachers of Buddhism, Christianity, Hinduism, Islam, Judaism, Taoism, and Native American traditions. He is the award winning co-author of Living Fully Dying Well (2009), author of InterSpiritual Meditation (2010), and producer of various documentaries on religion for the BBC and PBS.

Bastian is the former co-director of the Forum on BioDiversity for the Smithsonian and National Academy of Sciences, teacher of Buddhism and world religions at the Smithsonian, an Internet entrepreneur and translator of Buddhist scriptures from Tibetan into English. He is also an Adjunct Professor at Antioch University in Santa Barbara where he is teaching courses on Buddhism and Mindfulness Meditation. Bastian also teaches online courses as well as seminars and retreats at such organizations as One Spirit Interfaith, Chaplaincy Institute, CIIS, Sacred Art of Living and Dying, Interspiritual Centre of Vancouver, Cascadia Center, Esalen Institute, Omega Institute, Hollyhock Retreat Center, Garrison Institute and La Casa de Maria.

He is the Co-President of the Interfaith Initiative of Santa Barbara, co-founder of ECOFaith Santa Barbara and Trustee of the United Religions Initiative Global Council.

If you are interested in learning more about retreats, online courses and our mentor training program, please contact me at this email address: ed@spiritualpaths.net